4 CHILDREN, 3 BABY MOMMAS, 2 DIVORCES LATER

What I Learned from Failing in My Relationships

QUINTON D. MCDONALD

ISBN: 978-1-954297-96-8

Alpha Book Publisher
www.alphapublisher.com

Ordering Information:
Quantity sales. Special discounts are available on quantity purchases by corporations, associations, and others. For details, contact the publisher at the address above.
For orders by U.S. trade bookstores and wholesalers, visit www.alphapublisher.com/contact-us to learn more.

Printed in the United States of America

Accolades

"While battling breast cancer, I also had to accept the fact that I had a spouse (now my ex) who would not assist me while I was on my back with a double mastectomy. Crazy, right? Twenty long years of dedication but he felt that counseling wasn't an option for him because there was 'too much on his plate already.' Huh? 'Can you wait until I am better so I can handle going to court and such?' I pleaded. Crickets...

It was during this darkness that I ran into Quinton one day. He could see that I was barely maintaining a conversation with him. He saw my despair and spoke words of hope and healing into my then broken spirit. If I was in the dark, I guess you could say that Quinton was a headlight... shining lights on my tomorrow.

Quinton was both systematic and solution-oriented when it came to helping me figure out how to overcome my present challenges. I could tell his goal was for me to have the fullest life possible—even if my family was falling apart. I loved having a 'family' but it was killing me emotionally, mentally, and physically. I can see that now (headlights).

I departed from Quinton that day feeling more 'unstuck' and started to love me, fight the cancer harder, and focus on a new life, new opportunities, and new adventures. That was seven years ago, and he was right! Fighting for your yesterday is fruitless; fighting for your tomorrow is life changing. I am happier, stronger, and better for redirecting my focus. 'She' is a better me (headlights still on)!!! Thank you, Quinton McDonald."

~ Shelley Delaney

I was talking to a woman I really liked, and made the mistake of not being completely honest with her about something. Let's just say I was accustomed to "playing" females and didn't know how to turn it off. But, I wanted to. I'm getting older, and I was ready to get this relationship right. I knew Quinton was someone who had a lot of experience with relationships because he was always open about the lessons he learned through his failures, so I decided to get his perspective. And I'm glad I did!

My initial reaction was to play the situation off and make excuses, but Quinton explained to me that honesty against all odds was the best way to move forward. He asked me, how can I say I really like her if I can't respect her enough to be honest. Even if it means I don't get what I want, being upfront should at least earn her respect. Next he told me that after being honest, I have to put my actions to work and cut those bad habits out that made me only want to play. I followed his advice, and it worked! It wasn't easy, but by doing the work and being truthful, I reestablished her trust and today we are still going strong. Thank you Quinton.

~Gregory Christmas

This book is really well written and easy to read. Quinton is very reflective and honest about why his relationships didn't work and what it took for him to break those bad habits. The parts that resonated the most with me were dating/waiting for sex and waiting to say "I love you." Those parts really hit home... I can say that his book is for anyone seriously invested in working on being their best self, and/or looking and improve the quality of their next (or current) relationship.

~Latasha Essien

Mission

My mission is to influence behaviors and help develop understandings that directly contribute to people establishing more fulfilling, happier, and more long-term relationships. It is my opinion that if we change the way we view relationships, the way we get into them, and the way we act while in them, it can lower the amount of toxic relationships formed and proportionally decrease the divorce rate, especially that of African-American communities. As someone who has failed multiple times, my approach isn't to tell you what to do. I just want to explain what I did that didn't work and things I learned along the way that did. It may not work for everyone, but then again, if you really try, it might!

Another part of my mission is giving back to the community. Most behaviors are learned during our adolescent years from the things we are exposed to. I wouldn't be who I am today without the influence impressed upon me by positive mentors. Mentors who were introduced to me through the youth programs my mom registered me for. As a way to give back and to instill these lessons on relationships on the younger generations where it can imprint, I am partnering with Positive Atmosphere Reaches Kids (P.A.R.K.) of Little Rock, Arkansas. P.A.R.K. is an afterschool program that aids high school kids in everything, from homework to college enrollment. I will be donating ten percent of my total book sales from 2021-2022 to them in appreciation for what they've done for me and what they continue to do for the youth in our neighborhood.

Dedication

The one thing I always told myself was that I wanted to be a better version of my father.

Regardless of how that may sound, it is not meant to be a slight towards him. My father is a man who has multiple kids by multiple women. I'm his oldest, but I spent the least amount of time with him. Yes, I did see him enough to have some memorable moments, which I'm thankful for, but "moments" are not enough to feel like I had a present father in my life.

Back then, I didn't know much about the Laws of Attraction or how they worked. I just had an adamant desire to be better. Fast forward, and today I have four children by three different women, neither of which I'm married to today. Go figure that in investing so much energy trying to avoid it, I ended up becoming just like him in that aspect. However, I can say without a doubt that I've spent far more time with my kids.

But, it's not enough. Not by my standards, and it's even worse being in an occupation that makes it difficult to see them consistently: the military. Like me, my kids didn't ask to be here, and it is not fair for them to have a father who can't be there when they need him. With my two oldest kids, the impact that's been caused by me not being there consistently is apparent. Now that they are older, and more mature, they are asking those "hard" questions that further emphasize the impact of me not being there.

Another injustice that I've noticed about our community in general is we have a trend of living, working, and dying without hardly ever leaving something behind but grief and debt. As parents, there should come a point where we stop living for ourselves and start putting systems in place that will benefit our children. To call a spade a spade, it's selfish to have a mentality of "I figured it out, you can too." It is repressive and prevents our forward movement as a people.

Having said all of that, I dedicate this book to my children, Malachi, Mariyah, Gabriel, and Donovan. Everything I'm doing now is for you guys. I know that nothing can replace the lost time we've had to experience, but I'm working to make sure it was worth it. My dream is to be able to give you the world and afford you opportunities that will enable you to live your best lives. I want our last name to stand for something more than a fast-food joke. I love you with everything I am; I apologize for everything I'm not. This book is so dedicated...

Table of Contents

Chapter 1

Preface

*"If you want something you've never
had, you must be willing to do
something you've never done."*
~ Thomas Jefferson

Ladies and gentlemen, how much longer must we stumble through the process of being in relationships? How much longer do we accept outcomes such as disappointment, heartbreak, or regret because we keep getting it wrong? If you are reading this, then I hope the answer is no more. I hope you are at a point in which you are ready and willing to look at things from a different perspective and do things in a different way in order to get different results.

People in general are so complex that being in a relationship is inherently challenging. You basically have two completely different universes colliding. But that does not have to mean to be in one successfully is impossible. We see happy couples all around us. And if you are reading this, then like me, you may be asking,

"Why can't I find that?" Well, for the most part, we are going about being in a relationship the wrong way.

Whether it's due to a lack of know how, lack of effort, or our selection criteria, something we are doing isn't adding up. My goal here is to express some of these things, in hopes that if you can identify with them, you'll know what areas you need to work on to increase the chances of you finding your happy ever after. It will still be challenging, but gaining this understanding and acting on it should help things progress more smoothly down the road.

Now, if youagree that everything in life has processes, rules, or principles that apply to it, then understand that relationships are no different. You must approach a relationship with the frame of mind that it is a process, and like all processes, there are steps that should be followed to help it become more successful. Failure to acknowledge or complete these steps can turn dating into a game of relationship roulette where every time you meet someone you are playing a game of chance.

With that, one purpose of this book is to get you to shift the way you view relationships by first addressing yourself. That's right, you have to take a scrutinous look at yourself. This is where the buck starts and stops in the dating process. Ask yourself: are you ready, are you capable, are yourelationshipworthy? Answer truthfully! In my case, I absolutely was not ready, but I selfishly dove into countless relationships anyways. I used any means necessary to justify my actions internally so that I didn't "feel bad" about playing with someone else's emotions. The truth is that I lacked the discipline to deny myself the things I wanted and made myself blind to the fact that I needed to work on myself. Where I was vaguely conscious that I was making jacked up decisions, there are some who truly have no idea about the implications of what they are doing. They don't see it until it's too late.

This is because oftentimes people don't take the time to do a true self-inventory or take the requisite time to work on themselves prior to starting the dating phase. It's either people don't think about it, or like me, they do think about it but they lack discipline and/or are too selfish to stop from moving forward. But if you don't go through the process of fully understanding who you are as an individual, then how would you know what you want, need, or can contribute in terms of a relationship? How do you know if you are ready or even capable of bringing someone else into your life for real?

You can jump into dating and figure it out as you go, but how many failures and how much wasted time do you want to go through in order to learn this lesson? Keep in mind with this particular arena, failure has collateral damage (hurt feelings and emotions). This means that in failing to know yourself, not only can this negatively impact you in relationships, but it can open a gateway of negative trends for your partner as well. It can cause them to add defenses and insecurities toward the next person they date. That's how bad dating cycles are created. Even if you master everything else covered here, if you don't take the time to get yourself figured out, I believe it will be in vain.

Another purpose of this book is to get you to view a relationship as a process driven endeavor that takes time to solidify. The words "process driven" are used purposefully because that's exactly how you should see it. You have to think in terms of completing a series of steps in order to create something meaningful. That means it's going to take some work and time to do successfully. Know that the end result will be the culmination of how much care, time, and effort you put into the foundation.

Not all processes will be the same, but an important thing to note is that all processes need time. Yes, we live in a society that places emphasis on expedient results. However, this is not an area where we should expect that. Some things can't or shouldn't be rushed if we wish to accomplish them properly, and creating a relationship is one of those things. At the beginning of a relationship, as we will cover later, there are so many things happening in your mind and in your body that it's practically impossible to say if it's real or not without allowing adequate time to pass.

It's okay to be every bit of a hopeless romantic, but a great house can't be built in one day and a degree can't be earned in one semester. If you want your first relationship or the next one to be your last, then let the process take its natural course up front when building it to save time, energy, and potential heartbreak in the end.

The third purpose of this book is to offer different perspectives as they pertain to relationships. Sometimes when you are in the middle of a "situationship," it can be difficult to see things from outside your point of view. I speak freely on my experiences because understanding different ways to look at a scenario can help break you out of the tunnel vision and allow you to see a bigger picture.

Tunnel vision comes from looking at circumstances through a lens of persuasion (e.g., emotion). This lens has a tendency to put bias on the way you see things. However, if you can observe similar situations without that bias, you'll be more inclined to see it as it really is.

Two things I ask as you read this are: 1) try to be open-minded to thinking differently and actually trying the exercises, and 2) be honest with yourself when asking and answering the questions that will be presented. You have to stop lying to yourself before you can stop lying to others. My dad once told me that if you learn how to change people's minds, then nothing can stop you. Being a young boy at the time, I didn't get it. But now, I fully understand the challenge associated with this task. We are stubborn and don't like change even when we know it's for our own good. But we have to get comfortable leaving our own comfort zones because that's the only way true growth can occur.

I can tell you now, change isn't easy. Both of my marriages failed for some of the reasons covered in this book, and in my second marriage I actually put a lot of effort into trying to change. At least I thought I was putting forth effort. The fact is you don't know what you don't know, and I didn't know exactly where to apply the effort to save my marriage. I was still missing some faculties that would've made my efforts more effective and more sincere.

I also came to realize that I was trying to force the changes in order to provide immediate gratification. But when you force change, you will only get temporary results. It wasn't until I actually dedicated myself to improving through discipline, time, and consistency that those changes were permanently ingrained into my being. It'll take the same dedication from you if you wish to achieve the same. However, don't let the amount of work that will be required deter you from doing it!

It's funny that many people profess to want happy, fulfilling, and long-term relationships yet they shy away from doing the work. They want it to be easy and just fall into their laps. The truth is that the ability to be in a successful relationship is a skill. And like any skill, it requires study and practice in order to be perfect. Yes, emotion plays a part as we will discuss, but that doesn't mean to overlook the practical and technical aspects. These aspects are especially important when your emotions are being triggered which, as you should know, can happen from time to time in long-term relationships.

To really capitalize on having a great relationship, you have to continually fill your toolbox with things that support having one. This book is but one tool, and one tool will not solve all of your problems or answer all of your questions. This particular tool may not even be for everyone who reads it. I want to reiterate that people are so diverse there is no "fix all" solution. However, by reading more books, attending more seminars, and doing the work, you can fill your toolbox with items that can give you the best shot at success. If you are ready for this adventure and up for the challenge, then let us begin!

Chapter 2

My Story

"When you make a mistake, there are three things you should ever do about it: admit it, learn from it, and don't repeat it."
~ Paul Bear Bryant

"The first and best victory is to conquer yourself."
~ Plato

Yes... As the title of this book says, I do have four children by three different women and two failed marriages. It almost feels like my own rendition of the twelve days of Christmas. In that spirit, if I continued the countdown, then my "one" would be having a mission. That mission is taking everything I've learned in my experiences and sharing it with you in hopes of adding a perspective that can help your relationships fare better than mine did.

Getting to a point like this in life, having my circumstances, isn't something that happens overnight.

This is the result of years of having flawed thought processes which contributed to me making many bad decisions. Of course I am very proud to be a father, and I wouldn't trade my kids for the world. However, in hindsight, if I had been a more mentally mature person and stood on principles like integrity and truth, my life would be quite different today.

I had an extreme lack of discipline and a strong spirit of selfishness that caused me to make choices out of the pure desire for pleasure. There would be times that I knew I was getting myself into a situation that could turn out unfavorable, but I'd proceed forward anyways. It's a hell of a thing to know that you are doing something jacked up (e.g., playing with someone's emotions) but not have the discipline to stop yourself. And with a couple of my kids' moms, though I verbally sold a different story, my inner truth was I just wanted someone to be with for the moment.

My Past's Contributions

I grew up in a single-parent household with three brothers. Each of us had different fathers, and neither of them were present in our lives. I didn't understand it back then, but not having that male figure present in the household set some of the foundation for me becoming the person I did. The lack of having an example of what a man is supposed to be or only being subjected to bad examples growing up (like my mom's shitty boyfriends) is something that subconsciously influenced the way I pursued relationships.

I can't blame my actions entirely on that, especially as I got older, but it was definitely a contributor. And the impact was not only apparent in my relationships, but my brothers' relationships as well. We were legitimately lost when it came to art of long-term love.

The only thing I knew is that we werealways provided for. No matter what, my mother made sure we had food, clothes, and a roof over our head. So, when I got into my own relationships, more specifically my marriages, I figured as long as I was providing then I was fulfilling my role as the head of the household. I didn't have any other metrics to measure it to back then.

Something else that I feel affected me growing up was a lack of support from my family. Of four boys on my mom's side, and being the oldest of four on my dad's side, I never had any family come to support me for anything I ever did. Band, track and field, stage plays, spelling bees, FBLA conferences, billiard tournaments, etc. Even going into college, joining the choir, and joining a fraternity, no one ever came to see me perform.

When I saw how everyone around me had so much love and support in the audiences, I couldn't help but to feel abandoned and unloved from having no one there. In order to not feel sad all the time, I ended up creating an ideology in high school that nobody could do anything for me, but me. It sounds silly, but it made me stop depending on others to be there for me, and I became my own support system.

For the most part, it worked. By not expecting anybody to be in the crowd for me, I wasn't disappointed when they weren't. However, I'd find out later that there were still suppressed feelings from it. In fact, I remember venting to my mom these very thoughts when I was twenty-two years old, and I was mentioning a play I had been in when I was eight. She told me she'd come and didn't. What made it worse is that I thought I saw her in the back at one point, and I got more excited, only to be disappointed when I ran up to a complete stranger. Still, fourteen years later, the thought of that scenario brought me to tears.

Recognizing that you have pain points, even when they may not feel like pain points, is not an easy thing to do. And when you aren't even willing to open yourself to the idea, it's practically impossible. And it's one of the reasons people never seek help because they don't realize that something is wrong to begin with. Like I said earlier, you don't know what you don't know. So if you are reading this and you have been having trouble in relationships, don't be afraid to consider the not-so-obvious reasons as to what could be affecting you and, ergo, affecting them.

My oldest brother eventually figured it out. His advice was, since we understand we are at a disadvantage (having the lack of a male figure in the household), we have to take it upon ourselves to seek out the answers to our questions outside the household. We have to be willing to ask the question, "How do I become the man of a household successfully?" Whether throughreading books, taking courses, or talking to older men who seem to have figured it out, we have to learn that lesson. But without the desire or understanding that we are affected, many of us don't reach out until it's too late. And that's what I did. By the time his words hit home, I had already caused massive damage in my second marriage.

Take It and Run with It

Let's go back to my high school experience for a moment. This is where the bulk of my personality and my behaviors stemmed from. Remember, I felt that I wasn't getting support from my family. I had a father who was barely in my life, and the only consistent example of love I had was through the act of providing. Subconsciously, I adopted the notion that love equals providing. Ididn't know it back then, but whenever I look back now, that's exactly what was happening.

It was in high school that I found out girls thought I was attractive. It was an attention that I deeply leaned into. In some dysfunctional way, I equated their attraction to me with them caring about me, and it made me feel special. When I started having sex, this feeling intensified, and I started equating that attention to love. I know how it sounds now, but for a young teenager who equated love to providing and had a huge hole left in his life due to a perceived lack of support, it made perfect sense. I had finally found something to replace the "love" I believed I was missing. And even though they were temporary encounters, in those moments, someone was there providing for and supporting me in a sense.

Just to make something clear, my family wasn't horrible. I wasn't an outcast, or homeless, or anything like that. I just didn't like the fact that though everyone on both parents' sides lived in the same town, and nobody ever came out to support me in anything I did. It made me feel insignificant in a lot of ways. Nobody was ever there to cheer me on and show me how proud they were of me. They didn't even ask questions about how it went when they did see me.

Again, I'm not oblivious that this may not make sense to some of you, but these are my truths. Going from not feeling supported by my family to being a womanizer is a transition that may not compute to you, and that's fine. This is "my story." What you have to do is figure out in "your story" what are the factors (if any) that led you down the path of having toxic relationships. Only by discovering those things can you create a pathway to fixing them.

By the time I made it to college, it had become almost like an addiction to me. Chasing that feeling. In fact,

I can say it was no longer about making up for what I felt I wasn't getting, but more so about indulging in what made me feel good, period. Plus, I had gotten really good at it. To be transparent though, the fact that it wasn't relevant anymore didn't stop me from using it internally to justify my behavior to myself. It was the sob story I continued to perpetuate so I wouldn't feel completely guilty for the bad decisions I made or games I indulged in.

I can realize, understand, and admit that. What is something that happened to you as a kid that you have the power to overcome now, yet you continue to hold on to it? How much longer will you let that prevent you from moving forward? Not saying it's easy, but don't allow yourself to be hindered by it forever. Especially when you know better. There are avenues out there that lead to healing if you truly desire to get there. You have to get to that point where you stop blaming the past and start holding yourself accountable for why you are the way you are.

That's a lesson I alluded for a long time and because of that, during my college years I broke a lot of hearts. I was really good at running game and getting women to like me but sucked at actually following through once I had them hooked. I sold a lot of fairy tales and manipulated a lot of them, which I'm definitely not proud of, but that's the truth of who I was. I got to a point of doing anything I had to, saying anything I had to, in order to get to the point of winning them over. I called it getting into my "mode."

Marriage Number One

College is also where I met my first wife. I was twenty-one years old, and I had just moved back home to Little Rock, Arkansas, from Memphis, Tennessee, pursuing a career in acting and modeling. I decided to move back home and live with my mom for a year to save enough money to move to California. I was adamant about being a big-time movie actor and/or model. In the meantime, while working towards saving money, I decided to help my fraternity brothers with events on campus.

We were getting ready for a Black and Gold Pageant, and that's when I met her. The pageant coordinator, a really good friend of mine and mutual friend to us both, is the one who determined that one of the contestants and I would make a cute couple and should date. When I saw how she looked at me and knew there was a window of opportunity, I entered my "mode" and started playing directly into it. Within a month, she got pregnant. And within six months, we were married.

I didn't plan on any of that. I wasn't even looking forward to a future with her. My mind was still on moving to California. And I know this is going to sound messed up, but I wasn't even that interested to the point of being with her forever. I just played really well into the part since we were dating. Yet another example of my decision making, manipulation, and inability to be truthful with myself all because I was chasing immediate gratification. But when she got pregnant, I really did try to shift the way I saw our situation.

Remember, I told myself that no matter what, I never wanted to be like my father. I didn't want to have kids and not be there to raise them (look how wonderfully that worked out). So when she got pregnant, I pushed for marriage. She called it off about three times, but the salesman in me kept reeling her back in. In hindsight I know I was only interested in my own feelings of not being like my father, and I disregarded the reasons she may not have wanted to move forward, one of which was we really didn't know each other that well.

What's even more crazy is I have this ability to sense certain energies from the people around me. On the day of our wedding when I saw her crying as she walked down the aisle, I immediately knew they weren't tears of happiness. More than the events leading up to the day, I knew this was something deeper. So that night, while lying in bed I asked her why she was crying. She said she felt like she was making a mistake and wanted someone to stop it. Being that my initial intentions weren't the noblest, that shouldn't have surprised me, but it did.

This was just day one, and this caused me to already mentally check myself out. My "be better than my dad" blinders were off, and everything she was saying before finally hit its mark. I started wishing I didn't push so hard for marriage, because we could both sense the turbulent times that lay ahead. Our marriage was empty, and it was obvious we were just going through the motions.

I eventually ended up cheating on her with someone that I met on MySpace. I can't justify it, but back then I tried to. I figured that since I was with someone who didn't love me, wasn't there for me, why not indulge where someone was showing me attention and being there for me in ways that I needed. I reverted right back to the person I was in high school and my early college years. I went into my "mode" and pursued that attention. I would tell her about the affair years later when we contemplated on getting back together.

After our child was born, we tried to work it out but it was too little too late. We were already on the verge of crumbling because there was nothing in the foundation. Our breaking point came in a conversation about an off day from work. During that conversation, I saw a side of her that made me see her in a different way, and I'm sure she saw something different in me as well. I won't get into all the details, but things got really ugly really fast, and we realized how much we really didn't know about each other. We split up, divorced, and changed our focus on trying to simply be good co-parents.

And Then There Were Two

My plans of being a movie star and/or model had to be temporarily put on hold. I now had a child to support. So, I looked for a job that paid a little better than being a Dillard's sales associate and I became a car salesman. That's actually where my love of entrepreneurship came from. I fell in love with the idea of creating my own income based on the skills and effort I was willing to put in. I've always hated working beside someone, knowing we got paid the same regardless of who did more work or worked longer hours.

In 2008, for those of you who can recall, the economy went belly up. People couldn't pay their mortgages, let alone purchase cars. I needed to find something else to do to keep supporting my son. So I decided to join the military. It was an opportunity to continue providing for my son and make sure he had insurance coverage. I could also finally finish my degree and travel the world. It felt like a win-win all the way around at the time. While I was waiting to go to bootcamp, I continued to hang around my college campus with my fraternity brothers.

Anyone who truly knows me can tell you that my favorite game is pool. I've been playing it since I was ten years old, and it's something I got really good at it. The common area of the college's dormitories had a pool table, and I spent a lot of my time there. All the residents would want to play me, and sometimes I gave lessons. Enter my daughter's mom.

She saw me playing one day and complimented me on my skills. She asked if I could give her lessons, but I knew she was interested beyond that. Even though I knew I'd be leaving soon, I went into my mode and pursued that attention. I fed into it and pursued something romantic with her. You'd think that having a child now I'd do things differently, but I still never took the time to address those things in myself, thus my behaviors persisted. I knew I was laying it on thick, but in my mind, I was just wanting someone to have fun with until I went to bootcamp.

In my first marriage things were expedient. Everything happened at an accelerated pace. And in this case, I wasn't honest upfront with what I was looking for. The common denominator is in both situations I wasn't real with myself and lacked the self-discipline to control my urges to take advantage of the opportunity to be intimate with someone. I just kept pushing forward regardless of the reservations that popped into my mind from time to time.

A week before I left, we had unprotected sex. To be safe, I went to the store and got a plan B pill and took it to her job so she could take it. We didn't read the box in its entirety, nor did we research exactly how it works. We just assumed that it was good for 24 hours. So, that evening when she got off work, we were intimate again, thinking that we were still covered. When I got to bootcamp, about three weeks in, I got a letter from her stating that she was pregnant.

This was during the time my first wife and I were actually contemplating getting back together, so I became very defensive and denied that it was my kid. I brought up the plan B and was adamant that it was someone else's. That series of communication through letters drove a very big wedge between us. I was a blatant asshole, and she was a young pregnant girl who thought that we were going to be together and happy forever. We didn't really start healing from that series of communication until my daughter was around four or five years old.

Right When I Was About to Give Up (Marriage Number Two)

Now standing directly in the shadow of my father's footsteps, I started to do "some" self-reflection. I was now faced with the fact that I had two kids by two different women. My inability to control myself put me in the exact same predicament that I swore to avoid. My inability to be honest with myself and others about what I really wanted led to two women having my children, and I wasn't going to be there to help raise either of them because I was now in the military, and my ex-wife decided she couldn't handle the fact I had another kid on the way.

Despite this, I still didn't learn my lesson. When I graduated bootcamp and went to my basic skills training school, I went right back into chase mode. I hadn't "had any" for about two months and I was hungry. The new environment provided new opportunity and I was all too anxious to find out how much. I was doing the same things I was doing that led to me having two kids by two different women. One late period scare later, I finally got to the point that I had a revelation. I was acting insanely! I was doing the same thing over and over and expecting different results. If I didn't want to continue going down the road of surpassing the likes of my father, then it was time to change.

I made a declaration to myself and a promise to God that I was done. I was done chasing women, and I was done letting the pursuit of sex impact me the way it had. I started reading the Bible more in-depth and literally began to ignore women. My plan was to just focus on being the best father I could be from a distance. When I relinquished that need to chase, I literally felt a peace I had never experienced before. And for four days— SMH—I felt liberated.

While in school to learn my job for the Navy, I had one of the few designators that they allowed to bring cars on base due to how long the training pipeline lasted. Because of that, I was often the designated driver for my friends. Well, this one fateful night of driving around drunk people, one of them invited me to come inside this on-base bar. I really didn't feel like it and passed. Then all of them started egging me on, practically begging me to come to the bar. Another one even mentioned that there was someone they wanted me to meet, and again, I declined. As I was walking toward my barracks room, one of them grabbed me and said, "Just give it five minutes," and basically started dragging me with them.

I caved in and went to the bar. Inside I was introduced to the woman who would become wife number two. Our meeting was awkward because neither of us wanted to be there. We both got dragged in by mutual friends, and neither of us was really looking to meet anyone. To appease the drunks, we attempted to have a conversation, and over the course of the night we both got really comfortable talking to each other. When the bar closed, we had exchanged numbers, but she asked me one question before we parted ways, "Do you have children?"

In my mind, I was like, *Yep, that's it,* as I told her I had two children by two different women. She kinda made a sound of disappointment then walked off. Being that I had decided not to chase women, I was kinda relieved. I didn't expect to encounter her again. However, five days later she called because she needed a ride to the mall to get her phone fixed. To keep it professional, I charged her five dollars for gas money. Yes, I certainly did!

While waiting for her phone to be fixed, we grabbed a bite to eat and started conversing some more. That's when we really started to feel each other. We realized that even though we were from totally different places, Arkansas and New York, we had a lot in common. I even told her about my declaration to stop chasing women, and she confided she had made a similar declaration not long before I did. Staying true to that, I wasn't thinking about getting her in the bed. I was genuinely getting to know her.

For me, this was the first time I could remember connecting with someone, and it not be linked to some ulterior motive. I got to know her for her, and the more I learned the more it appeared we had in common. After about three to four weeks of consistent three-to-five-hour-long conversations on the phone, adventurous dates, and getting to know each other, we decided to enter into a relationship. That was the first time we had sex.

This is where I learned the importance of not letting sex be a driving factor when getting to know someone. I'll talk about this more in detail in the chapter on dating, but in short, when you have an agenda, the connection you are making is influenced to meet that agenda. When you don't have one, you can establish something unbiased and genuine. And in case you were wondering, having a real connection made the intimate part so much better.

Other than a few hiccups, things were going great. I even convinced myself that she was my reward from

God because I had finally learned to stop chasing women and meant it. After a year together, I got orders to get stationed overseas, and a little bit of panic set in. I didn't want to lose this awesome woman who was beautiful, could accept me for who I was, what I came with, and our relationship which was still blossoming. Looking at how quickly things progressed in my past marriage, I figured a year was more than enough time to be solidified, so I pushed for marriage.

Up to this point, the "hiccups" we had encountered were around finance and women from my past that I was still friends with. Finance was an issue because I was an E-3 in the military trying to balance paying two child supports and maintaining all my other bills—car, insurance, phone. So there were times she had to pay for dates or help out in other ways. I remember one time she even paid to get my car out of the pound. Smh...

Women were an issue because even though I had been sexually involved with a few of them, I literally just saw them as friends. Understandably, she wasn't comfortable with me being cool with women who had experienced me in that way. I became defensive because some of them I had known since I was a kid and our families were long-term acquaintances. Not to mention she still had her guy friends (even though she had not been intimate with them). In hindsight, I showed back then that my priorities were messed up. If she was the woman that I professed to love and wanted in my life, then after I stated my case, if she still felt the same, I should've just respected it.

Not to mention her family wasn't too thrilled with the idea of her marrying a man with multiple kids to begin with. I had to have a couple of conversations with her mom, but when she saw how serious I was about her daughter, she eventually gave me her blessing. This was a new territory for me, and I can say for a fact that because of the way things progressed I actually had real love for this woman and wanted her in my life. I just sucked at proving those words with the proper actions a lot of the time.

I wanted to marry her because if something happened to me, I wanted her to be taken care of, and I also knew if I went overseas under the status of being married I could make a lot more money. I told her that we could build a nest egg to launch us into our new life together. But that selfish reason of not wanting to lose her was still a strong motivator as well. We thought about it, talked about it, and decided to take the step to get married.

Love is great to pour into a foundation, but it is not enough. To make a marriage last the distance, there are more tools that you have to obtain and a mentality you have to develop. I had still never taken the time to figure these things out and though I loved her, I didn't address my ability to be selfish. I still didn't know what it meant to be a good husband, to sacrifice, and to not get complacent. Because things started off great, I thought we'd go the distance, but over the course of the next seven years, I would find out just how important those other faculties were in a relationship.

We only had the chance to live together for one month before I left. Both being in the military we figured we'd have to be away from loved ones, but thinking it and living it are two different things especially so soon. However, like adults we were ready to take on the challenge, get it past us, then move on to living our lives together until the next assignment.

When I got to my duty location, it was immediately hectic. The danger was immediately apparent, and I immediately questioned why the heck I agreed to take on such an assignment. I ended up making a circle of five friends, and we became each other's stronghold. We did everything together. Remember I said one of the hiccups my wife and I had was female related. Well, two of the people in the circle was a female, and one of them was gay, so...

I'll admit that, among all of us in the group, she and I got a little closer than was appropriate. I used the fact that I had a limited amount of people to hang out with as justification, but there is no excuse for crossing certain boundaries. We'd watch movies together alone, come to each other's rooms, work out together, eat together, almost like dating. One day she posted something on Facebook, not saying my name but referencing her "special friend" who helped her pass her physical fitness test, and my wife's radar lit up.

Even though I knew some lines were crossed, I tried to justify us just being friends because of our circumstances. As messed up as I know it is now—and that's just part of being selfish—I didn't want to let go. I held on to my reasoning for wanting to keep the friendship all the way up until the young lady said we needed to create some space. The thing is, she was married as well, and her husband was now getting uncomfortable with our "friendship."

When I told my wife that we were going to create space because her husband was getting weary too, she got really mad. She didn't understand how I couldn't take her feelings into consideration, but the young lady could take her spouse's into consideration. I couldn't say anything. There's only one truth: I was selfish and my priorities weren't aligned with being a married man. Though I never admitted the lines that were crossed, I know my wife could feel it and this deployment changed our dynamics. What a way to start off a new marriage.

My inability to not be selfish continued to lead to many more issues. It eventually got to a point where she felt that I took her for granted, was consistently inconsiderate, and, in her words, was downright mean. I couldn't see any of that at the time. In my mind, we were fine because we went from a one-bedroom apartment to a two-bedroom apartment, then to a four-bedroom house. We went from no kids to having two kids, and they were both being provided for. Again, my definition of love was providing, and I was doing that. So despite her telling me time and time again that she was feeling a certain type of way, I didn't heed her words because I thought we were more good than bad.

It was when we hit the age of thirty that she started to reflect on her life and didn't like what she had seen. She had sacrificed a lot for our relationship to work and didn't feel appreciated for it, so she decided it was time to leave. Unlike the other times where I could talk her back, this time she was truly done. She even put some things in motion to make sure I couldn't talk her into staying. I think this situation was her first time actually seeing me cry, and I mean bawl my eyes out. I really couldn't see the things I was doing as that bad to warrant that she leaves me.

Needless to say, I was devastated. Everything in me hurt. There would be times I'd be cleaning the house and find a sock over here or a toy over there, and I would be reminded that my family was gone. The pain would hit me all over again, but I had to face the fact that it wasa bed I made for myself. Though I would go through the next few months trying to mask the pain I was feeling by chasing women, ultimately this was the catalyst for my change. To give you a glimpse of the mindset I was in, this is a poem I wrote a month after she left:

"My name is Quinton McDonald, and I know that I'm a catch. In fact, I don't believe there's many women who can qualify as my match. I wear my slacks and button ups, blazers and square toe shoes. I have a whole collection of watches, and colognes that smell good too. I strut around with my chest out, and my head held high. I think I'm being confident, but it comes off as arroganceand pride. See underneath this fabricated exterior, I have inner demons that always rumble. You can't tell me that I'm wrong, and I find it difficult to be humble. People around me always saying Quinton humility is a must, but bump what the things they're talking about, I'm the only one that I trust. See I carry this chip on my shoulder, and this personality has become ingrained. I couldn't even change it when it was causing my wife pain. Yes, I said wife, 'big bad' Quinton got married. On top of that we have two beautiful boys that in her womb she carried. My wife BY FAR is the best person I've ever known, and despite all she'd do right, I'd continue to do her wrong. See this pride thing is a bitch, I took her for granted just knowing she would stay. I never thought I'd be in an empty house, because she took the kids and went away. Was it worth it to always be right, to always win, thinking there was something to prove? So set in my own ways, I neglected every chance I had to improve.

My wife wasn't meant to be my competition, my job was to show her she already won. If I could do it all again that's how I would've treated her from day one. And now I finally get it, but I've already had my one last try. My ego completely deflated I see I'm nothing, without them by my side. For anyone going through something similar, listen to these words without any doubt. Drop your pride and gain humility before you lose everything you care about."

Never Feel That Pain Again

This was the first time that I experienced going through the stages of grief to this extent. And I hit them all. Denial, anger, bargaining, depression, and acceptance. My stages didn't happen in that particular order; they bounced all over the place. Basically, I was confused. The only thing I could think to do to steady my mind is get back to what I was used to. I created dating profiles on five different dating apps and became a dating monster. My divorce wasn't even final yet, but it was the only thing I could think of at that time to mask the pain I was feeling. In hindsight, I should've used that energy to fight harder to get my family back. I can't tell you to this day why I didn't... I allowed myself to just feel and accept defeat.

I became reckless. During this period, I went on more dates than I'd like to admit. My mode was in full effect. I was spending money I didn't have and bedding women left and right because I didn't want to face my reality. I didn't have the maturity to confront myself or look at myself in the mirror and address the things that were causing me to act this way. During these escapades, I had even gotten two women pregnant. Both of them decided not to keep the pregnancies, but what if they had? That would be six children by five women! Those scares finally gave me the motivation to embrace the fact that it was time for a real change.

I finally stopped running from processing my emotions and started to deal with them. I again tried to see if I could salvage my marriage, but you know what they say about when a woman is fed up. It also didn't help that I told her I had started dating. Her reaction made me believe that potentially there was a chance if only I had really, REALLY tried. If I had gone all in to show her that my family did mean everything to me.

It's worth noting that during the time of my separation, I was actually dealing with several stressful circumstances at the same time. That's not to justify my actions but to paint the picture of where my mental state was. Let's just say if I wasn't as resilient as I was, I probably would not be here right now. I was dealing with getting scammed out of $3,000 when I tried to find a roommate to move in with me. That led to me having to move last minute and find a cheaper place to stay. I was trying to figure out how to get my car fixed from an accident that had just occurred. Lastly, I was facing disciplinary action from my job due to accusations from one of my recruits on my professional demeanor. It felt like I was being hit from every angle.

I sank into a very deep depression. I couldn't stop crying, my performance at work was lacking majorly, my finances were in shambles, I almost had two more kids by my own recklessness, and I didn't know how to come out of it. Every day I was crushed by my failures as a father, a husband, and a man. One day, while looking in the mirror, I didn't like what I saw. In fact, I was disgusted with myself. That day I had two options: take myself out or improve to never feel like that again. I decided to improve because the other option would've just perpetuated my selfishness. I still had four kids to think of. And please don't take this as me playing the victim. I got exactly what I deserved, and I understand that I created my own hell through my own flawed decisions.

Now being "scared straight," my next problem was I didn't know where to start to achieve real change. I didn't know how to be a man who had his stuff together for real and wasn't just pretending. If my desire was to ever have a family and to sustain it, there were a lot of tools I needed to acquire. My brother's words resurfaced: We have to be willing to ask the right questions and seek out the answers via any mediums available. In other words, it was time for me to humble myself and ask for help. The first thing I could think to do was counseling/therapy. So I got a therapist. Next, I turn to the internet. More specifically, YouTube. I developed a habit of watching three to five videos a day on the topics of self-improvement, success, and love. I did this every day for eighteen months.

I started reading books dealing with those same topics, and that's also when I got more into the law of attraction. I attended seminars and did some research where I spoke to several people around me who had been married for a while. I asked them questions like how they make it through tough times and what the secret is to their longevity. I asked the men what it meant to them to be selfless, and to live for someone else. I had to immerse myself in the process of becoming a better person and truly understanding relationships.

Over the course of this eighteen-month period, I did these things relentlessly, and I noticed that my mentality started to change. I noticed that the way I perceived things started to shift. And eventually, it just clicked. Things like being selfless, priorities, "happy wifehappy life," sacrifice, unconditional love, and communication all just started to make sense. I could now replay moments from my marriages and see all the wrong I did on so many levels. From things I said to the things I did. Some things were so obvious I'm still in disbelief I didn't recognize I was doing them. It's crazy how sometimes you really don't notice how negative someof your actions are when you convince yourself you have good intentions. It won't be until you shift your thinking and remove that self-bias that you can look at them for what they really are.

During this period of transformation is when my divorce was finalized. I wished more than anything that I had reached my revelation sooner, but I also firmly believe everything happens for a reason. What my evolving thought process allowed me to do was accept my new reality with a higher level of understanding about how we got there. I was able to let go and focus on moving forward with less of a weight on my shoulders. And I continued to improve myself so I could be ready to form more meaningful and healthy relationships down the road.

My Path Forward

When I decided to get back into dating, I noticed an immediate difference in how I looked at women, how I approached them, the things we would talk about, and what I wanted. I was no longer searching just for sex, and I was no longer willing to accept it from those I had no true desire to be with. I was dating with my mind and my heart, and that alone was able to influence how conversations and interactions progressed. It also allowed me to look deeper into the person across from me beyond their external attributes. This is where I learned the power of not only knowing who you are and what you want, but what it means to date with a purpose.

Now don't get me wrong, there are some times when an intimate encounter can be a good thing. Just be honest and communicate that up front. Don't blur the lines of being intimate with someone and wanting to be in a serious relationship with them if that's not your intention. As the saying goes, "You ain't got to lie to kick it." Be honest. I promise you someone will be on that page with you.

On the other hand, when I did meet someone and we hit it off, I was more confident we were interested in each other for the right reasons. We would communicate effectively, actually enjoy each other's company, and it would be apparent that it wasn't just a physical attraction. Being able to connect on multiple levels and having great chemistry made the sexual connection that much better when it did happen. Now my relationships were ending for circumstances outside of our control, versus ending because I wasn't honest. For instance, being in the military, it's hard to expect someone to uproot their whole life and follow me around the globe.

From that experience, I learned that even when things are going well, that still doesn't mean that a person is for you. There is so much more to take into consideration. There are just too many variables to guarantee anything. However, by having healthier relationships consistently, you increase the chances that when you find the one who will go the distance, a solid framework will already be laid. In the event it doesn't work out, there will still be less pain than if deceit or manipulation was a factor. There will still be hurt feelings and disappointment, but there is a difference between something failing due to deceit, inconsistency, and/or someone not being ready, versus failing because as time progresses you realize it's just not compatible or circumstances create an obstacle.

Ultimately, the big thing for me was I got to see that all the work I had been putting into myself worked! I was approaching relationships much more maturely. As someone who started off as a villain and transitioned into a man of good character, I got to see the best and worst of both worlds. You can say this shift caused me to develop a sort of an intuition when looking at other relationships. I was able to clearly see patterns that were toxic or behaviors that were bound to lead to the relationship failing. I was also able to use my experience at failing to suggest ways others could succeed. And nine out of ten times when someone took my advice, their relationships pivoted for the better... even if that meant not being together.

Now that I have the proper frame of mind and a new understanding of what it means to be in a relationship, I want to use that gift in conjunction with my experiences to help anyone I'm able to. If I can, I want to prevent someone from making the same mistakes I did that led me down my earlier path, which eventually led to deep depression, sadness, and heartbreak. I hope that my story and the things I've learned along the way would be enough to deter someone else from following that same pattern. The world does not need more fatherless babies. And I hope that people will be able to form more fulfilling and long-lasting relationships moving forward.

It is not easy. Again, it took me eighteen months of pure dedication to this process, and I'm still working towards being a better person every day. It takes conscious effort and a desire to improve, but you can do it. Don't let yourself suffer continue to suffer under toxic relationships before you actually get it. Don't be like how I was, a 32-year-old little boy who was pretending to be a man. Take the things I'm writing here and actually apply them.

I failed over and over again before I could succeed. This book contains the lessons, insights, and perspectives I've learned along the way from those failures. If you are a person like I was, still trying to figure out what being in a successful relationship really entails, or if you just want to find ways to make your current or future relationships better, then I hope at least some of the words here resonate with you. Even if you are a woman reading this, the concepts covered are universal and can help you as well. I want to thank you for taking this journey with me, and I hope your final destination is as bright as mine.

Exercise:

What's your story? Take the time to actually write it down. See if you can pinpoint some things that may have contributed to why your relationships have been the way they were.

Chapter 3

Addressing Self First

"You've got to be willing to die to who you are
now to give birth to who you can become."
~ Les Brown

"Mastering others is strength.
Mastering yourself is true power."
~ Lao Tzu

There was so much I didn't know or understand. There was so much I didn't prepare for. There were so many tools missing from my toolbox. I just assumed that being in a relationship would be easy. At least I convinced myself they were or why else would I have jumped headfirst into two marriages? I mean, yes, as I mentioned there were times I thought about the fact I wasn't as interested as I portrayed, but I didn't have the maturity or discipline to walk away before things got too deep. I purposely ignored all those signs because of my selfish desire to have someone in my life. If I had taken the time to really reflect on those thoughts and evaluated myself truthfully in terms of being ready for a commitment like marriage, things would've turned out differently.

Relationships are formed in this same manner every day. We secretly know that we aren't ready or that we don't fully understand what being in a relationship entails, yet we proceed forward out of our own selfish want/need to be with someone. Or, equally bad, you say yes because you don't know how to say no. But, having selfish thoughts such as only thinking of what you stand to gain in being with someone, in and of itself is a tell-tale sign you aren't ready to be in a relationship. No matter how much you like someone, how attractive you think they are, or what they can provide you, you should never jump in a relationship prematurely. Nor should you jump in one because it's convenient or because you want to avoid the feeling of loneliness.

It's also important to make sure before bringing someone else into your world that your world is in as much order as possible, starting with having the right mentality. You have to do an honest inventory and recognize if there are any character flaws, personality traits, and/or leftover emotional scars nesting inside of you that can be detrimental to being in a relationship. Trying to find and fix these things while in a relationship leaves the door open for negative side effects to fester. That's because, one, change doesn't happen that easy, and two, nurturing a new relationship takes enough energy as it is.

What this means is that your focus will be divided, and you won't be able to fully commit to self-improvement as much as you think you will. What usually happens is that you get complacent or comfortable, and the need to work on yourself diminishes. You revert back to the behaviors you are used to and begin to re-establish patterns that led to your previous failures. Thus, the cycle continues, potentially leaving more broken hearts in the wake.

It's crazy when you think about it. How this cycle of brokenness can perpetuate more broken people, especially when one of the reasons why relationships end in breakups is because one or both of the people in them are broken in some form. That's why I strongly believe in acknowledging these areas prior to entering into a relationship and then taking the time to actually work on them. This will put you in a position to be a better partner and end the cycle (by removing that avenue of brokenness) the next time you do bring someone into your life. But to do this successfully, it's going to take some time. How much time really depends on you, how honest you are with yourself, and your overall dedication to healing.

The biggest bump you'll have to get over is removing the false narrative you tell yourself on a daily basis. You know, the one that shrouds you from the type of person you really are. The one that helps you justify the bad decisions you make with some seemingly noble reasoning to help you feel better. I'm sure we can all agree it's not easy to confront certain things about ourselves because they'll make us recognize how imperfect we are. However, for this process to work, you can no longer ignore these things or treat them like they aren't as impactful in your life as they are.

Sometimes these false narratives can also fool you into thinking that you have more control than you do. That you have the ability to change your behaviors whenever you want to. It's kind of like those who say they can quit smoking whenever they want, yet five years later they are still smoking. They don't want to admit that they have an addiction, and they package this self-deception as a choice to feel more in control. However, you won't be able to create a desire to change things that you don't acknowledge as problems.

Don't shy away from the fact that you have weaknesses under the belief that if you don't admit them then they don't exist. That would be like thinking an illness will disappear if you just stop talking about it. Instead, embrace the fact they are real, and use that acknowledgment to have something tangible to fix.

I don't want to come off as saying this is easy to do because it is not. It mayevenrequire seeking professional help in order to uncover some of the things embedded deep within you. But if you are serious about wanting to obtain a more fulfilling and happy relationship, addressing your issues is an important part of that journey no matter what.

The Dilemma: Inside Looking Out

The truth is many people don't look at themselves and think, *What do I need to work on to improve myself today?* We just go through our days, living moments as life occurs and accepting the outcomes of the decisions we make. I know for a fact when I was at my worst, I wasn't thinking in terms of how I could do things differently to improve. Especially not when it came to dating. I was just searching for someone to have beside me with no set criteria or intentions in place.

When one ended, I was on the search to find the next one to fill the position. I remember there were times that some of the women I dated tried pointing out things I needed to work on. But being in a place where I wasn't ready to face my demons just yet, it was easy to become highly defensive and reject the idea that I was the problem. I'd come to find out that more than not being ready, there were two specific attributes I possessed that prevented me from being able to accept my own faults: pride and ego.

These two culprits were powerful in preventing me from being able to concede certain truths about myself. Not only were they detrimental in my relationships, but they also negatively impacted multiple areas of my life. And I wasn't alone. There are a lot of people impacted by these two negative attributes. But, whether it is pride and ego, denial, or a host of other factors, the point is that there are many reasons for someone to suppress their flaws in order to convince themselves they are better than they are. And when it comes to relationships, you can only keep the real you suppressed for so long. It may help you land the relationship, but it won't allow you to maintain it. Plus, if you are willing to lie to yourself this hard, how much more are you willing to lie to someone else?

For those who can recognize they do have unresolved issues, get help if you are unable to overcome them alone. Sounds easy, but here lies the dilemma... Just like I mentioned earlier, admitting inadequacies to yourself can be seen by some as embracing a form of weakness. From my experience, this more so applies to men. A lot of men are predisposed via society to think they have to adhere to a certain code of masculinity. A masculinity that makes it bad to openly show weakness. Now, this doesn't apply to everyone but many misinterpret what it actually means to be masculine.

In many black communities, more specifically, there are a lot of young men who don't have an example of what male masculinity is even supposed to be due to the absence of many black fathers in households (much like myself). So we try to figure it out on our own and stumble along the way. Through trial and error, the examples around our neighborhoods, and what we see on TV, we try to piece this concept together.

I eventually discovered masculinity does NOT mean the lack of vulnerability or weakness. Those who hold on to this misinterpretation think it's "weak" to admit needing help. In fact, it's quite the opposite. It can take a great deal of masculine energy to be vulnerable. Yet, instead of being humble and asking for help to address the root causes of their problems, they compensate by concocting false personas. Personas they use to cover up their insufficiencies and to try to control the perception of who they want people to think they are.

The only thing this creation does is make it even harder to admit your faults because now you've compounded the layers. As the notion goes, one lie leads to another lie, until you live in a web of them and they become a reality that's hard to break free from. But it doesn't have to be a lie. You have the ability to become that person in actuality if you choose to. First, destroy your web of lies and face yourself. Some things have to be broken down before they can be built back up, and the breaking down is never fun. But on the other side, when you are essentially reborn into the person you envisioned, it will have the genuine feel that was missing when you were pretending.

For me, my main façade was portraying that I was more financially well off than I was. I would spend copious amounts of money that I really didn't have just to hold on to that perception. I mean, what man wants to admit he's broke? Especially when he has kids? The inability to be honest with myself and my need to create this image were so powerful it sent me into massive amounts of debt. In hindsight, I saw that if I would've just taken those hits to my ego and sacrificed the want to chase women for immediate gratification, I would've gotten to financial stability much sooner.

This mentality isn't just prevalent in relationships though. I'm sure we all know someone who spends money recklessly in order to present a more elevated status. Spending rent money just to keep up with "the Joneses" for example. I realized that holding on to that perception was so important because of my desire to have companionship, and I knew being broke wasn't attractive. I carried this lie for years, even at the cost of not being able to do more than the minimum for my kids. And all just to get women, some of whom I can't even remember now... but I remember not being able to send extra money to help my children sometimes when it was requested.

That feeling of guilt—and this is just for me—wasn't a proper penance for not being able to do more for my kids. I felt like a piece of crap. And to think if I had just taken the time to really work on myself, address my finances, and have the maturity to understand what was really important in life, I wouldn't have desperately compromised myself as many times just to go on dates.

As a result, I could've actually become the man I was pretending to be, been a better provider for my kids, and saved SO MUCH money in the process.

A good question is, what other issues or insecurities are out there that people are hiding under a false front? What other behaviors do people have a hard time confronting? At what point do we stop pretending and actually work toward being? Life is not a game with a reset button. It's real, and a person's deeper emotions are real as well. At the end of the day, most people will know if they are ready to be with someone or not. It's something that can be felt in your "heart of hearts." If you aren't ready, can you not be selfish or inconsiderate long enough to not play with someone else's emotions by bringing them into your web of lies?

The Dilemma: Outside Looking In

As I touched on earlier, there are also a select few who truly don't realize that they have things they need to change. They've exhibited certain behaviors for so long that it's become normal for them. Have you heard the term "nose death"? Well, people can have behavior death as well, where everyone around them can notice the problem except the individuals themselves. It's hard enough to change behaviors you can identify as being problems, so imagine trying to change ones you are completely oblivious to.

For people like this, they may have to look more externally to find the areas where they need to improve. We've all heard the adage that the devil is in the details. Well, if those around you continue to sing the same tune about you, and the things they are saying aren't positive, then maybe you should pay attention. Just because you can't see it yourself or you don't agree with it doesn't mean it's not there. That's the thing about perception—it belongs to the beholder.

If multiple people around you are noticing the same things about you, then at some point you have to accept your role as the common denominator. You have to accept that even if you don't agree with them, something about you is making them see you that way. And if it's a recurring theme, you owe it to yourself to figure out why that is. Either that or just hang around new people. Now, don't think you have to take everyone's inputs and run with them. There are obviously those who don't have your best intentions at heart. But those inputs coming from close friends and family—those you trust—may be worth taking a look into.

Getting defensive, like I used to, is counterproductive in one major way. That is, you miss an opportunity to gain insight about yourself on things you may not have noticed before. Being defensive is a close cousin to being mad, and if everyone is entitled to their opinions, why are you letting theirs get you upset? Is it because it may be a little true and you don't want someone calling you out on it? Or is it because you are so set in your ways you reject the notion of someone telling you otherwise about who you are? If it's neither, then embrace the fact that someone's opinion is just that—theirs. Again, if these critiques are coming from someone who has merit to you, then inventory them open-mindedly to see if they hold water. Otherwise take them with a grain of salt.

The bottom line is that change is necessary no matter how you get to it. Don't let the dilemma of societal expectations, self-imposed fallacies, pride and ego, or the inability to accept constructive criticism distract you from the ultimate goal. It's going to take putting conscious effort into this process for it to be successful. If you allow its difficulty to cause you not to overcome this challenge, you'll miss the rewards that lie on the other side. Not only that, but if you can't make the changes necessary to be in a successful relationship, you run the risk of perpetuating a system of failed relationships leaving behind a trail of brokenness.

The Self-Audit

If you are open to the idea that you have things you may need to change, the next question is how do you go about starting the process? Identifying your faults is one thing but addressing them is another. There is no set answer as everyone's process will vary, but for me I had to get to a point of being utterly disgusted with myself before

I started. Hopefully, you don't have to get to that point before you start yours.

For me, first I had to remove my biggest distraction and stop dating. I decided to give it up while I embarked on this journey because I didn't want to be lured back into the same pattern of thought processes and decision making. Next, I had to look into the mirror and confront myself about the things I wasn't readily able to accept. I was selfish, argumentative, inconsiderate, non-supportive, mentally abusive, mean, and a user. Even though at the beginning of my process I couldn't see some of those things clearly, those were words I continuously heard so I allowed them to hold weight.

I made it a point to find out how much it weighed by truly getting to know myself beyond the mask I presented to everyone else. And the more I confronted myself, the more I became increasingly comfortable with accepting that I had these nasty faults. I thought outside of my biased frame of reference and started to see things through her eyes, and there it was. All the things I'd done that were in alignment with having those negative attributes were slowly becoming more apparent. It eventually became so plain that it made me sick to my stomach.

All those mixed emotions of anger, disappointment, and feelings of failure that I previously suppressed resurfaced, and I used them as fuel to drive my desire to achieve true change. Looking at myself in total transparency, I was not ready to have that inner conversation. But I did it anyways. I asked myself questions like, *Who am I? What type of man am I? What are my values and principles? What do I have to contribute to a relationship at this point? Am I ready to bring someone else into my life and build them up mentally, take care of them emotionally, love them unconditionally? Why did my last relationship fail? What personality traits do I have that are inherently detrimental to having a happy and successful relationship? Am I still holding on to past hurt (either from a past relationship or childhood trauma)?*

I've asked myself questions like these before but only on a surface level where my fabricated persona could provide the answers I wanted to believe. Answering them in this new state returned completely different answers. Not as kind and pleasant but exactly what I needed to continue confronting and improving myself. Most of the things I was told I needed to work on, I was now able to see and understand clearly. My therapist helped add understanding from a different perspective and helped me uncover things that I didn't pick up on. Again, I can't stress enough the importance of seeking help, and not trying to do this all on your own.

A therapist is professionally trained to help guide you to the source of why you've developed certain behaviors or thought processes (i.e., things youmaynotevenrealize impacted you). They know methods and techniques that you've probably never heard of that can help you gain access to, and understand, information about yourself essential to improving. Remember, getting help is never a sign of weakness. Talking to counselors, therapists, or psychologists for the betterment of your mental health is never a bad thing, whether it's for you as an individual or done as a couple.

The important part of true change is giving it time. How much time largely depends on how much you have to fix and how honest you are with yourself. This may sound easy, but I assure you it is not. Even though I got to a point where I could clearly see my faults before I engaged internally to ask myself those probing questions, I still had to check myself on some of the answers. Change doesn't happen overnight, and you have to remain cognizant of if the answers you are providing are the truth. When you've lived a lie for so long, it's not easy to just reverse it. The mind likes to stay in character. So you really have to focus and break through the superficial answers—the ones you know are genuine.

As an example, let's examine one question together. What are your values and principles? When initially reading this question, what are the first thoughts that come to mind? Like me, did you think: honesty, integrity, family, hard work, trust, loyalty, etc.? Most people will think these things because they are in line with how we all WANT (the bias) to see ourselves. These are the attributes most of us were raised to exhibit, and they are characteristics that society paints as noble and belonging to a "good person."

However, what do your ACTIONS (the true self) say about your values and principles? Meaning, is everything you do in accordance with being those things? Or if you do a deep dive, would you discover that you don't work as hard as you should, you've lied more times than you'd like to admit, and/or there are things you enjoy doing more than spending time with your family? There are definitely those for whom statements like these are more realistic. They are just hard to admit or accept because they generally aren't socially acceptable, and/or they force you to realize how imperfect you are.

But understand that doing things that don't align with the principles you want to uphold doesn't make you a "bad" person. It's more normal that you'd think for people to think one way but behave in another. It's something many people struggle with daily. Don't beat yourself up about it. The harm is in when you recognize this pattern then consciously decide to continue denying it. I said it once, and I'll say it again: You can't change something that you aren't allowing yourself to identify as a problem. Once you accept it for what it is, then you can start the process to fix it.

The Three Parts

This section is based solely on an ideology that I subscribe to. You do not have to adopt it. It's just what I use to illustrate the "why" behind it being possible to think and value certain things but not act in ways that align with those things. This ideology isn't new, and more than likely you've heard of it at some point. I'm referring to the concept that people are a compilation of three parts: mind, body, and spirit. This is a concept that greatly helped me grasp control of myself. It taught me to be conscious that these three parts exist and how to cultivate each of them to work in harmony.

Self-control defined means being in complete charge of your own emotions, thoughts, and behaviors. This translates directly to the need to have control over all three of these areas. Mastering this concept is something that some people spend lifetimes in pursuit of and still struggle with. It is not easy. But simply having an understanding of it can put things in perspective enough to help you gain more self-control. James Allen, in his book *From Poverty to Power* says, "Even a very partial success in self-mastery adds greatly to one's power..." My goal here isn't to teach the theory behind this ideology but simply to help aid in that understanding.

As a scenario, have you ever told yourself you wanted to do something the next day, like go to the gym, for instance? But when the next day arrives, you don'tfeel like going or you can't find the motivation or energy to get up and actually go. What results is either you don't go and feel bad about it afterwards, or you do go and feel a sense of achievement that you did it. Also, if you went, you might've even realized that despite not wanting to go, you actually had a better workout than you expected. You would've thought you'd be sluggish, so why weren't you?

In short, this disparity exists more times than not because your three parts aren't in alignment with each other. And since they are each their own entities, they can stand independent from one another. This also means they can work against each other or in harmony with each other. Where one part may be pushing you to do something to move forward, the other two may be holding you back or adding contradiction. Where your mind may try to convince you of one thing, like in our example, your body can be completely the opposite, and vice versa. However, in harmony, they all work together to help you move in the direction you set. It mostly boils down to how you've been conditioning yourself over the years.

Are you someone who is accustomed to saying you are going to do something but often don't follow through? Do you often engage in negative self-speak, such as "I can't do this"? Or are you someone who does the things they set their mind to regardless of how they feel? It's all relative, and it all aids in the conditioning of your three parts.

Now apply this ideology to relationships. You may tell someone you love them and actually think you mean it, yet you entertain the first attractive person that comes your way and/or shows you attention. Or you may realize that you lie to your partner about things from time to time. In these scenarios, you may be conceptually in love with your partner, but your body is still searching for other sources of fulfillment, or it could be the other way around. You may love the physical aspect of your relationship but mentally be elsewhere. And your spirit could be the guilt you feel for knowing you aren't all the way in it the way you should be.

There are plenty of books out there that can give you a way better understanding of how these parts work together and things you can do to condition and strengthen their unity. Find two or three and read them. One that I'd recommend is *Soul, Mind, Body Medicine* by Dr. Zhi Gang Sha. Again, I'm no expert on this, but I can vouch that being aware of the relationship between the three parts and the correlation it had on my ability to have better self-control was very apparent. And having increased self-control made me more disciplined in relationships.

Other Things to Consider

Let's change gears for a second. I think by now we can all agree that working on ourselves mentally, emotionally, financially, and spiritually are extremely important. But there are other avenues that are involved with working on yourself that are equally important, two of which are life experience and skill sets. In short, other than being internally a "good" person, what do you bring to the table that can add to the value of a relationship?

Thisgoesformenandwomen. Howareyouatproblem solving? How are you at conflict management? How are you in terms of taking on and handling responsibility? Can you cook? Are you a good housekeeper? Are you a good provider? Just like it takes more than love for a relationship to be successful, it also takes more than just having a sound personality to add substance to it. Have or develop tangible assets as well.

Think about this... Up until eighteen years old (older for some), you've depended on someone to take care of you and make decisions for you in some capacity, be it your parents, other family members, guardians, teachers, mentors, etc. Even if you claim to be someone who grew up in circumstances that forced you to mature early, that care (whether recognized or not) was still in place to some degree.

It's really not until youembark on your own in life that you really start to see what you are made of. That's when you really get to define who you are as an independent person and put into practice the lessons you've learned along the way. Anyone who's had any type of formal training can attest that learning information is night and day from the actual application of it. This means even if you were raised to be self-sufficient, until you get out and start doing it, those skills won't be sharpened.

However, if you go from an environment where you were always being taken care of, straight into seeking a "serious relationship" (which is finding someone who will in turn continue to take care of you in some capacity), you forgo the process of learning what it means to take care of yourself. This may not be the case for everyone, but in general, going through this "alone" phase has great benefits. It's where you develop those other assets that will enable you to contribute more effectively to a relationship. It's where you learn to be comfortable, self-sufficient, and develop confidence as a single person.

Now, honestly speaking, what do you bring to the table? The more you can contribute, the more valuable you are. I've seen too many situations where one of my male friends was a great provider, but he sucked at being a supporter, a listener, a partner, and in handling responsibility. He only had the one skill set of earning income. I've also seen a lot of female friends who think that beauty should be the only thing they bring to the table. They can't cook, upkeep a house, or contribute to expenses.

Some people may cherish these things, and having a person short term who is financially competent or physically pleasing is great! But in the long term, it will never be enough. Partnership is about mutual contributions in several areas. While you are taking the time to work on yourself, make sure you include building yourself up with life skills and experiences that add to you becoming a more well-rounded person. Make sure you have something more than the bare minimum to offer.

In my story, the first time I lived by myself was when I was thirty-three years old. Other than that, I was either with my mother, with a wife, or with roommates. I was able to learn how to set up bills and manage a household from my marriages, but I didn't know what I was missing outside of that until I finally lived alone. Yes, I was a great provider, but I had nothing else. I didn't realize how much growth I was missing out on until I lived by myself. Even at thirty-three, I was able to mature a lot! This led to me being truly comfortable for the first time as a single and independent man. I learned to love my own space, and I became cautious of the people I allowed in it.

This unknowingly became the final phases of my transition. I was collecting missing pieces that I didn't even know I was lacking up to this point, and I could finally look in the mirror and start seeing that man I had envisioned so many times before. I even taught myself how to cook. When I started to date again, I noticed yet another shift in the way I viewed relationships. I wasn't worried about finding someone who was going to accept me with my circumstances. I had reassurance of the value I still brought to the table and was no longer in a position to just accept anyone.

Having that sense of certainty about myself, I started to attract women at much higher calibers than I did when I was the "pretender." Not only that, but I was no longer pressed with the feeling of needing companionship. I was able to take my time and actually get to know someone, which did allow me to save a lot of time and money without feeling like I was missing out on something.

Becoming more complete as an individual and being happy with yourself should not be overlooked in regards to its impact on being in a healthy relationship. There's an old adage where people say, "I want 50/50." I don't agree with that; it should be, "I want 100/100." Where one complete person seeks another complete person to make a 200% product. Please do not confuse this with having to become perfect. Perfection is not the goal. The goal is simply being a better person who is fit to be in a relationship. Once you have the right habits, understanding, and mindset in place, any growth from that point forward will be in the right direction, including a majority of the growth you will experience with your partner.

To sum this section up, it's worth quickly noting another benefit that comes from working on yourself: the establishment of your own authentic identity. Knowing who you are. There are people out there who, if you don't know who you are, will try to mold you into their image. And this is something that happens quite frequently. Even if it's not intentional, you can subconsciously pick up on someone else's patterns of behavior more easily when your own isn't in place. Influence is ever present, and this one piece of the equation can determine how susceptible you are to it.

Of those who purposely try to mold you, who's to say they have the best intentions for you? They may be molding you to be dependent on them to help fill some insufficiency they are facing. They may use your lack of identity as a weapon to try and control you. "You ain't nothing without me," "I made you," etc. If you know who you are, you know your worth and you won't have to worry about venturing down one of those paths.

Discipline Is a Must

While going through this process, you will be faced with plenty of internal obstacles. I believe the best thing to do in order to control external obstacles is refrain from dating. Dating has a great potential to complicate things and potentially slow down your progress by blocking your focus. Go into your process expecting these sentiments. Yes, it is going to suck. Yes, you are going to feel like you are missing out. Yes, you are going to feel alone and empty at first. However, by staying the course, trust that you will find light on the other side.

Don't worry about or be afraid of the sacrifices you will have to make in order to achieve your change. Hold on to the image of the person you are becoming, and exercise the discipline and consistency to get there. Unfortunately, that may include having to let go of a current relationship if you know it's toxic. There is no fix for being with the wrong person. THERE IS NO FIX FOR BEING WITH THE WRONG PERSON. So if you weren't the person you needed to be when a relationship began, and as you grow you notice that this person isn't conducive to who you want to be, you have to take action.

Have the discipline to walk away in order to further your growth. One thing about humans is that we are emotional beings and creatures of habit. That's why it doesn't matter if a connection is good or bad. When we have to sever ties with someone, it always leaves a sore spot. But success in anything requires massive actions. It requires making yourself uncomfortable. You may not see your destination vividly while going through the trials and tribulations of the transition, but don't stop or succumb to those doubts because it is definitely there. Trust the process, and the results will follow.

The expression goes, "If it were easy, then everyone would do it." Well, it's easy to give up or stop trying, which is why there are so many people having relationship problems. You can become one of the few who decide to do what is hard. Les Brown has a saying, and though he meant it as a business philosophy, it can apply here as well. He said, "You must be willing to do the things today others won't do in order to have the things tomorrow others won't have." It's hard to tell yourself no or deny yourself instant gratification. But in doing so, you are building a character trait that is beneficial to being successful in anything. You are training yourself to have discipline and to be in control of yourself. And by doing these hard things, you'll be rewarded accordingly.

Again, we are creatures of habit so even in saying all of that, there will still be some who may find it impossible to just stop dating altogether during this process. To them I say, be prepared to have a longer process, and be cautious of losing yourself back to the habits you are trying to break. One way to do that is to be completely honest and transparent with the people you date. Tell them the truth—that you are currently in the process of working on yourself and aren't ready for anything serious. Tell them you just want to have fun.

Break the habit of telling people what you think they want to hear just to get close to them. Stop painting pictures that don't exist with your words and actions when you know your heart and soul aren't there. If you just want sex, say it. More people will respect you for that than you think. And even if being that straightforward doesn't lead you to accomplishing your goal, you still win because you are showing your maturity by not resorting to misleading or manipulating someone. Other than the temporary hit to your "ego," nobody really gets hurt.

What the Outcomes Could Be (With and Without Change)

One scenario that happens quite often is two people who've never taken the time to go through this process of self-improvement becoming a couple. Either one or both of them are broken or lacking in some capacity. The different variations of what this could mean are numerous and differ from person to person, but the fact remains that something they need to be good partners to each other is missing.

And when you don't have the capacity to look inward to see how your "stuff" may be causing relationship drama, a common thing to do is blame external factors (e.g., your partner) for things that are going wrong. When two people are pointing the finger back and forth because they didn't take the time to work on themselves, and as a result can't accept responsibility, it creates an atmosphere of tensionandhostility. Not to mention, when the realization that life isn't easy arises and now they have to compound the difficulty of trying to figure life out while also trying to figure each other and themselves out, even more chaos and confusion can ensue.

Unfortunately, this is still one of the most common relationships out there. People who are not ready, jumping in and out of relationships in a trial and error format, hoping for the best. The only basis they have for wanting to be with someone is usually attraction or infatuation. Yes, they may try to make short-term changes to accommodate the person they are with, but how long until those changes start to unravel? Without doing what is necessary to make those changes an actual part of your personality, when things like complacency set in, your true nature will be revealed.

If these are the implications of not being internally ready to be in a relationship, then what are some of the issues that can arise when what's missing are those other contributing attributes? As we mentioned earlier, what if they aren't contributing beyond money or looks? What if they've been in so many relationships with people who are willing to accept that bare minimum that they can't realize in order to have something real, more is required? Are they capable of contributing to the emotional, spiritual, mental, physical, or financial value of the relationship?

Just think, if one person is bringing 80 percent to the table and the other is only bringing 20 percent, eventually the one giving 80 percent is going to burn out. Or maybe the one giving 20 percent falls into a pattern of dependency, meaning they rely on their partner so much they may miss opportunities to grow themselves. Or worse, they are practicing usury and taking advantage of a situationship. Even though the saying goes, "Opposites attract," that doesn't apply to how much someone is willing to put into a relationship. Because another saying is, "Be ye equally yoked." It may not ever be truly equal, but intent goes a long way. How many times have you seen someone who "seems" to have their life together dating someone who "seems" like they are headed nowhere? This is an extreme case, but this imbalance is generally why.

To be fair, we have to acknowledge that people are so diverse there is no one scenario fits all. Without knowing people, you can't really say what the background is that brought them together. But when speaking on people you do know, I'm sure you've seen situations where one person is giving more than the other, further along in life than the other, more mature than the other, etc. What causes people who are considered good catches to pick these partners that can be considered badcatches? Do they just have good sex? What else? And don't get me wrong, I am not discrediting the value of companionship and friendship. Those are very important contributions, and if you are considering spending your life with someone, they are a must. However, thinking in a long-term sense, are friendship, companionship, and sex enough to fulfill you for the rest of your life?

Speaking only from my experience with the people around me, it goes right back to the theme of this chapter—working on yourself. When you commit to doing this, somewhere in this process you start to develop confidence and a higher sense of self-worth. It's like how I went from being worried about finding someone to love me while having four kids by three women to knowing I was someone still deserving of an amazing woman.

At first, I didn't care if someone brought anything else to the table as long as they were willing to accept my circumstances. This caused me to get into a lot of relationships where I was giving everything and they contributed little to nothing in return. Not even effort. But I accepted it because I felt "lucky" someone was choosing me. Now, having an established sense of worth, I expect a lot from the person I'm dating. I don't accept less than what I know I deserve, and I give just as much. From this space, you won't accept less either.

Another possibility why you may see couples who seem to be on opposite ends of the spectrum is people wanting to stick to what they are used to. This means that even though one person's life may have blossomed, they will still be attracted to the type of person they've always dated. They don't consider that they have the option of increasing their value. Now there is absolutely nothing wrong with liking what you like. Do you. However, if the relationship is constantly toxic or you realize you are supporting this adult like a child of yours, when do you raise the standards of the person you are dating?

It's also understandable that you may have grown up around people who influenced your "type," which gives you a very high level of comfortability with them. But don't sacrifice your mental peace or a chance to have something healthy because you can't step outside of your comfort zone. Remember you are reading this book for a reason. And if being in a healthy and happy relationship means picking a different type of person, then at least consider it.

You have to stop getting into relationships with people who may not have your best interest at heart. Or with people who take you for granted and won't be able to truly appreciate you. People who will take more from you than they are willing to give. People who just treat you like an option and are only interested because you are the one here right now, or it's convenient. Vice versa, don't be the one choosing someone just to fill a void, and definitely don't be with someone who doesn't make you happy. All these scenarios—and these are just a few—are more probable when you don't work on yourself first.

Now, how might this play out with two people who have gone through this process? This means people who took the time to address their flaws, established being comfortable in their single season, and fell in love with themselves. People who established their identity and developed themselves mentally, physically, spiritually, financially; haveall of their affairs in order; and acquired some life skills and experience along the way. First, a person like this is going to approach dating completely differently. Because to them it's not just about having someone to fill a space; it's about having someone who can add to or reciprocate the value they bring to the table and can appreciate who they are as a complete person.

These people are at peace with their circumstances and aren't pressed to have someone enter their lives. They are patient. They can take the necessary time in getting to know someone and only move forward when ready. By no means am I implying that dating from this spectrum would be perfect. Of course, there are still problems that can arise and of course, there are other factors that need to be taken into consideration, like a person's true intentions, which we will cover in the chapter on dating. However, starting with this type of foundation can greatly increase your chances of finding something more meaningful.

Exercise:

If you are ready to start the process of becoming a better person more suited for being in a successful long-term relationship, then do these two exercises.

1) Discipline Test: Set a goal for the next two weeks, and make it something that you know will challenge you. Whether it be refraining eating certain foods, going to the gym, working on a business, talking to family members, etc. Set it and do it daily for two weeks. Record your progress. See if it was something easy or hard for you to do. Use that as a base line to determine how disciplined you are and build from there. Get to a point where your discipline is solid.

2) Self-Assessment: Ask and answer a combination of the following questions. If your answers aren't to your liking, don't sugarcoat it. Embrace it, then figure out what you need to do in order to change it. Even if it requires seeking out professional help, do what you have to in order to become a better person.

- What does a relationship mean to you?
- Who are you? What kind of person are you (selfish, compassionate, mean, nice, etc.)?
- What are your values, morals, and beliefs?
- What do you want/expect out of your partner?
- What do you have to offer a partner at this point in your life?
- Are you ready for a serious relationship, or are you just wanting to have fun?
- Are you ready and capable of handling the responsibilitiesthatcomewith tellingsomeone you love them and want them in your life?
- Are you emotionally, financially, and mentally mature/stable?
- How much effort have you put into making yourself a good person/mate for someone?
- Can you say that, inclusive of everything about you, you truly love yourself?
- If you've answered in the affirmative for everything above, are you lying to yourself?

Chapter 4

Communicate from a Place of Understanding

"The biggest communication problem is we
don't listen to understand. We listen to reply."
~ Stephen Covey

I was in Pensacola, Florida, to attend recruiter training prior to a new assignment. Some of my classmates got together and decided to do a weekend trip to New Orleans. I called my wife, let her know what the plan was, and that I wanted to be a part of it. She asked if everyone in the class was going. I told her no, it would only be like seven of us. She asked why everyone wasn't going and I told her some people weren't interested in New Orleans, and others decided to stay in their rooms over the weekend and talk to their spouses. She responded with a "hmm." I told her I really wanted to go because it was an opportunity to do something I have never done before. Her response was, "If you think it's a good idea and we can afford it, keeping in mind we just had a baby two weeks ago, then go. You gon' do what you want anyways."

I really didn't think anything much of that scenario. Until we got divorced, that is. She brought it up and told me that it was a very selfish act to take that class trip, given our circumstances (newborn baby and financial plans). The last thing on my mind was that I was being selfish because from my side I made sure it's something we talked about. And whether I agreed with her or not, I had to understand she also had a side that made sense to her. If my goal would've been to see things from her point of view versus just to get my way, things would've turned out differently.

In this scenario, there were several opportunities for more effective communication that could've prevented this from being a negative staple in our relationship. The fact that it didn't happen is due to several reasons, internal and external, from both of our ends. From my side, I figured having the conversation was enough to put us on the same page, and her "giving in" was an actual greenlight. But I was listening from a point of influence by something I really wanted to do. I failed to pick up on the context clues in what she was really saying. On her side, she figured that if my priorities were in order, it should've been a no-brainer to not take the trip. So she became passive and failed to communicate directly how she felt about the situation.

Men are from Mars, and women are from Venus. We literally think about things from different places. Yet we tend to assume that the other gender can sense how we mean the things we say. There may come a time where you know someone well enough to read between the lines, but you can't always rely on that. You have to be very clear and direct about what you want to say, especially when it's something big. That's the only surefire way to prevent a misunderstanding.

Communication Basics

From something as easy as deciding where to eat, to something as complex as articulating feelings, communication is not easy. There are those who spend years learning to be effective communicators and still have trouble from time to time. The goal of this chapter is not to make you a communication expert; it's simply to introduce some tools and perspectives to help you understand it a little more. Introducing you to the tools is one thing, but it's up to you to actually put them to use. Effective communication is a skill that many people don't put enough effort into getting better at. Yes, it is a skill, which means you can learn it and/or practice to become better at it. There are some who do have a general understanding of how to communicate but still fail to do it consistently. This is even truer during times when this skill is needed the most. Those times are when there is a high degree of emotion involved. During the times a person's emotional state is elevated (i.e., anger, sadness, anxiety, frustration), the ability to properly communicate how you feel can get diminished.

When this occurs, it's hard to find the "right words" to say, and it becomes much easier to just speak from the emotion. Think about the times you are angry. Are you usually trying to figure out the best way to express your anger using some well-thought-out communication technique, or do you pop off saying the first things that comes to mind? Acting out of raw impulse provides the path to the least resistance, which means it the easiest way to go. Again, practice makes perfect, and if you try to implement communication techniques daily, you can create new natural impulses.

With that said, don't just read this chapter without actually trying to put the concepts covered into practice. It will only improve the way you communicate and help you better understand why others may communicate the way they do. Eventually, you'll notice that even at times when you are angry, your initial response and ability to process your words will be more controlled.

Before we dive in, let's do a quick recap on what communication is. Communication is defined as the exchanging of information or news between two or more entities using mutually understood sounds, signs, and symbols. It requires one body to construct a message, a medium to transmit the message, and another body to receive and interpret the message. The receiving body can then respond or simply act on the message received.

Communication can be verbal, non-verbal, or written. Each of these mediums can carry a different feel and should be chosen carefully based on what the sender wishes to relay. For instance, we've all heard that it's bad to break up via text messages, right? Why? Because text messages for the most part are impersonal and typically don't relay proper tone or emotion. When dealing with someone that you've shared an intimate relationship with, emotion and tone are important to achieve closure.

Using text messages to end a relationship signifies, whether you want it to or not, two primary things. One, you never truly cared about the person or their feelings to begin with. Or, two, you took the cowardly way out and couldn't face them to end things like an adult. If neither of these statements reign true, then using this kind of medium may not be the best way to express yourself in this type of circumstance, even if you have grown to dislike them. If at any point you did share something special, end things in a way that respects that. Verbally.

In that regard, I'm sure we can all agree that talking is the most common form of communication, but keep in mind it encompasses more than just speaking words. There are other elements that surround what you say that can impact the meaning behind it. Things like tonality, body language, facial gestures, word usage, and even actions play a part. Understanding this can help you be more conscious of what you are communicating not only with your words but with everything else as well.

Expect this—even when you do everything you can to express yourself in a way that you feel represents exactly how you feel, one thing you have to keep in mind is the receiver. That is the one part of the equation you can't control. No matter how you mean it, the receiver is still going to receive and interpret it based on their own perspective or level of understanding. And also, in those instances that they do know exactly what you are saying, that is not synonymous with having to like or accept it.

That means you have to allow that even when you are clear, concise, and honest, people still have the right to be angry, upset, or disappointed. You can't be like, "Well, I told you the truth so you should be happy." What if that truth is, "I cheated on you"? This sounds like it should be common sense, but I've seen people get mad because their honesty wasn't readily accepted by others. I used to be one of those people.

Lastly, we have to take into consideration how communication can really affect a relationship. Communication is effectively placed among the top three reasons for relationship failure alongside finances and infidelity. You'd think that would cause people to stop and pay more attention to this area, but in general we don't. We continue to look at it as something less significant than it is in terms of its impact on relationships. If more people truly understood that a majority of the arguments they have are simply based on some type of miscommunication, maybe they would reconsider.

Instead, what usually happens is two people who don't have a good grasp on effective communication start talking at each other. The result is that they tend to communicate mostly from emotional states, and when they listen, it's from a place of apprehension or defensiveness versus empathy. With each person only considering their own perspectives, arguments are bound to arise. Yes, disagreements are a part of life no matter how prepared you are. The difference is that when you understand effective communication, you have the tools in place to better handle those situations.

Yes, even without this preparation you can get to a point where eventually an argument seems to subside. But, without resolution the root is still there. That'swhy— and maybe you've experienced this—each argument tends to get gradually worse than the previous one. Each argument compounds on the previous unresolved argument over and over until a breaking point is reached. This leads to many relationships having arguments that never truly get resolved. It also leads to small things becoming huge things.

Why It's Not Easy

Like I mentioned earlier, there are distinct differences between the way men and women communicate. On top of that, those differences exist among each of us individually as well. It's our diversity. We all come from different backgrounds, family structures, experiences, education levels, cultures, etc., so the way we perceive information is different as well. It's why you can put together a carefully worded message, saying things exactly the way you want to, and it can still be misinterpreted by the receiver. Whether you realize it or not, that "detailed" message you sent was still a reflection of your views and understanding of the subject. The receiver will process it according to theirs.

That's why an important communication skill is learning to see things from other people's point of view. When you understand why the person you are communicating with sees things the way they do, not only can you customize a message so they'll better understand it, but you'll also receive their messages more clearly. The first step is embracing the thought that differences exist though. There are 7.8 billion peoplein the world who are all as unique as our fingerprints. Don't expect everyone to think, communicate, or understand like you.

Diversity—difference—is also driven by factors like demographics, culture, heritage, and social circles.

More internally, it can come from morals, beliefs, and personality types, to name a few areas. Each of these things has the ability to cause someone to interpret information a certain way. Additionally, some of these areas contain more than one facet by themselves. For instance, according to the Myers-Briggs personality test, there are sixteen different personalities alone.

But difference doesn't have to be a bad thing. There is great power in diversity if you learn to harness it properly. When many heads come together, offering their unique perspectives, we can create solutions to problems on any scale. The same is true for handling problems in relationships. A disagreement is an opportunity to understand each other more and ultimately make things better by collaborating together on a solution.

My second ex-wife is from Brooklyn, New York, and I'm from Little Rock, Arkansas. It goes without saying that we would perceive things differently. Our entire upbringings provided us with different experiences that shaped the way we think. That difference was more than just geographical as we would come to learn. Our entire family structures were different as well.

If we had taken the time to fully understand the way we communicated, or learned each other well enough to understand what was being communicated, then the scenario in the beginning of this chapter could have had an alternate outcome. Instead, we both did a lot of assuming. I assumed she was really okay with me going on the trip, and she assumed that I would look past her words to see that she wanted me to get my priorities in order. I'm a literal person, so telling me to go (nomatter the delivery) is telling me to go. She's a figurative person, and she figured that if my priorities were in the right place, it should've been common sense to not go and use that time and those resources to make things easier forher.

Now, if you can grasp the magnitude of how many different perspectives are out there, then it should become silly to think that there is only one way to look at a piece of information. Yet there are those who can't help but to embrace a one-sided ideology—those who are so ingrained in their own programming that it is the only reality they can subscribe to. This is why it is gravely important to know the person you are communicating with. Learn them. Learn their background. To increase your ability to understand what someone is saying, you have to be familiar with how they receive, interpret, and relay information. Develop empathy. It takes time but eventually, you will reach a point where you start to understand.

To better illustrate the concept of differing perspectives, take a piece of paper and draw a "6" on it. Sit across the table from someone and place the number facing you. You will always see the "6" and they will always see a "9". Based on your perspectives, you are both right and you won't see it any other way unless you both trade places.

It works the same way with communication and looking at circumstances or situations. We can only understand information based on our perspective. The things we've learned and the things we've gonethrough in our own lives shape this. Personal experience is the first place we can draw from when making a correlation to something. If everything I've experienced tells me this number is a 6, then I can only see it as such. If you try to convince me it's a nine, then all my defenses start going off. Or, I can try to relate and figure out why you see it as a 9. Once I'm able to relate, put myself in your shoes, I'll be able to see it too. This simple process can alleviate so many disagreements.

However, simple isn't the same thing as easy. It's difficult to break a lifetime of programming and be empathetic to someone else's views. It requires great discipline. More than in relationships, this concept of perspective and living in our own worlds is apparent throughout any circumstance. You can see it in the views between black people and white people, democrats and republicans, rich and poor, even differences like short and tall. Most people can't easily set aside their views to empathize with another enough to understand them. They tend to think that by doing so, they are conceding their own views and accepting someone else's. This isn't true. You can respect someone's views, and seek to understand them, even if you don't agree with them.

Never forget: It's OK to agree to disagree.

This underlying belief that if someone has differing views from our own, then it must be associated with some form of negative energy has to stop. As we've covered, it's okay that we think and see information differently as we are all... different. Who said that communication can only result in tit for tat, win or lose, or right or wrong outcomes just because differing views are present?

Communication isn't a battlefield where it has to be one over another. It's plain to establish the relaying and understanding of information. If these two things are accomplished and there is a mutual respect of the viewpoints expressed, then even if neither of you ultimately agrees, it's still a win. Just make sure you've expressed yourself thoroughly enough, taking into account how they receive information, to be confident that your message was received as intended, then leave it there.

Most times when someone expresses a reluctance to accept and agree to disagree on an outcome, it's because they feel like they aren't really being heard or understood. They feel that if you "really" knew where they were coming from, then you'd see it their way too. The best way to put those concerns to rest is to listen attentively and be able to restate their concerns to show that you do understand what they are saying. Once they feel completely understood, they'll be more receptive to the reasons you don't agree or see it differently.

The Purse Incident

Say this out loud: All disagreements don't have to be arguments, and all differences don't have to mean conflict. There's a saying, "Choose your battles wisely," meaning you don't have to make everything a fight. A lesson I learned a little too late.

I took my second ex-wife shopping for her birthday. We went to one of her favorite stores, Michael Kors, and I told her she could buy any purse she wanted. As soon as we walked in, I could feel how excited she was. She walked around carefully examining each bag. She eventually landed on this little clutch and lit up as she started trying it on and talking about ways she could use it. I asked her if this was the one. She said yes, so we headed towards the counter.

En route, we passed by this oversized bag and her face lit up even more. She placed the clutch down and started talking about all the ways she could use this bag instead. In her description, I zeroed in on the words "diaper bag." She just said she would be able to double down and use this $400 purse as a diaper bag. I wasn't a fan of that plan.

I immediately voiced my discontent, and it gradually turned into an argument because I didn't want to concede to her using the purse for baby products. From my point, I wanted her to understand that if she wanted a diaper bag we could go buy one for $30 at Walmart.

What she wanted me to understand was if the bag was for her, it shouldn't matter what she used it for—it's the one she wanted. By the end of it, what was supposed to be a joyous birthday occasion became one of our relationship's hell points.

In hindsight, I realize that I had every right to voice my opinion on using the purse in a fashion that could mess it up, but when she was adamant it's what she wanted I should've let it go. That would've been the perfect time to agree to disagree and move on. My opinion would've been heard, and she would've been happy, and we could've moved that situation into the "good memories" column.

When revisiting this scenario on my road to betterment, I asked myself, *Why couldn't I let it go? Why did it matter so much to me what she used the purse for, especially after telling her to get whatever she wants?* I concluded that it was my pride and ego that made me want to control the outcome toward what I wanted instead of really homing in on what she wanted.

Obstacles to Clear Communication

Our recurring theme of pride and ego strikes again here as they are big-time killers of effective communication. Communicating with one of these as your foundation can automatically put you in a state to be difficult, defensive, or one-sided. When your ego is heavily involved, usually the primary goal becomes to express how you feel or how you see something, and there is little to no room to allow anyone else's perspective. You think you are the smartest person in the room and that your way is the best way. When pride is heavily involved, then instead of listening to understand, everything that is said in contradiction to how you feel becomes an attack against you and you become defensive.

Both of these can be combated with just a little bit of humility. You don't have to be the smartest person in the room and even if you are, you don't have to let it be known. I can't count the amount of times I've heard partners in relationships say that they don't feel valued. One cause of this is feeling like they aren't being heard, or they are being made to feel that their opinions are invalid. I know I've done it as well. There were so many times I could've earned positive points with my ex by simply taking her inputs and showing her they were valuable to me instead of shutting them down in proper asshole fashion. I could've not only made her feel valued but also trusted and respected just by listening, removing my pride and ego, and embracing her inputs.

The crazy thing is some of us are so autonomous with how we communicate we don't even realize that we do it. You have to be conscious, and you have to be present with what you are saying to your partner. That means also taking into account the perceived communication.

As someone who is very logical, I did not do well at understanding what the perceived communication was behind things I said or did. For instance, logically, I didn't want my ex to use an expensive purse as a diaper bag, but the perceived communication from her was that I didn't value her choices or really care about what she wanted to be happy in that moment.

Another obstacle to overcome in communication is assuming. When you assume, you take half the information and mold it into a whole conclusion. You essentially rob the other person of the opportunity to conclude for themselves. Most people do this when they think they understand someone better than they do or know more than they do. Yes, there may come a time when you know someone well enough to predict how they will respond to certain situations. But even being right nine out of ten times doesn't mean they can't surprise you. There is a first time for everything.

Remember we are so diverse that any combination of feelings or circumstances can impact how someone feels at any given moment. So if you know someone well enough that they've consistently shown you who they are, then by all means prepare for and expect certain responses. But I would caution against acting on those expectations too expediently because this could be the one time they do or say something different. Allow that extra time and patience to let someone conclude their own points before doing it for them.

When it comes to relationships, assumptions can lead to blowouts. One reason is because assumptions can influence the way you communicate. If you assume that your partner will have a negative response to a conversation, you may approach the conversation already on level 10 in preparation for what you "think" you are going to receive. So when they match that energy, you feel that you were right when really you made them amp up with the way you approached them. You didn't give them a chance to show you how they really would've responded.

Another example is when you assume the meaning behind actions, especially when the assumption is negative. Because if you are wrong, you can destabilize the foundation of trust that your relationship is built on. In my first marriage, my wife started being really sneaky with her phone. One day I asked her what she was hiding and she kept saying nothing. The more I asked and inquired, the clearer it became she was hiding something but she wouldn't tell me what it was. I assumed whatever it was, it was bad, and accusing her of wrongdoing created a rift in our relationship. I eventually found out that she was just planning a surprise birthday party for me and didn't want me to find out.

In hindsight, there were so many things I could've done better. One, know the woman I was married to and understand that she wouldn't do anything to hurt me. That would've prevented any negative assumptions. Two, I could've trusted her and when she said nothing, I could've left it at that instead of reading more and more into it. Three, I could've directly communicated my concerns to at least have given her a chance to clearly state there was nothing inappropriate going on. Not all partners have the best intentions in mind for their mates; that's on you to know the type of person you are dating and to act accordingly. But when it comes to making assumptions, don't be too quick to jump to the negative side of things without proper validation.

Though there are others, the last obstacle to effective communication that I'll mention here is fear. Fear can range from having reservations to actually being frightened, both of which can impact how openly someone chooses to communicate. One thing to note is that fear usually develops over time. People get programmed to experience these feelings, whether it be through childhood experiences, past relationships, or current circumstances. If your interaction with someone is mostly negative every time you have a conversation, then you'll start developing reservations about things you want to discuss with them and may choose to avoid certain topics altogether.

People who are overly defensive, argumentative, abusive (mentally or physically), or narcissistic excel at making people feel this way. Unfortunately, these types of people don't readily change, especially not on their own. So if you feel that you can't openly communicate with your partner from any level of fear for what the response may be, you may want to reevaluate your relationship. You should not feel like you can't address certain concerns with the person who says they love you.

I've only named a few things, but there are literally dozens of other variables that can serve as obstacles in communication. And they are not mutually exclusive—they can be used in tandem. Let's take assumption and fear for example. Yes, making some assumptions can lead to fear, especially depending on how negative the responses have been historically (i.e., hostile or violent). At that point, assumptions are made on the side of safety.

But some assumptions can invoke unwarranted fear and create a situation where one wouldn't have existed otherwise.

More than fear of response, there is also fear of consequence. For instance, knowing you should tell your partner you cheated on them to maintain integrity but doing so will more than likely cause the relationship to end. Not wanting to face this consequence, most people will take these types of secrets to their grave. I mean there really isn't a pass for betraying someone's trust to that degree, but if two partners have established a communication pattern based on being open, honest, and understanding, then they may be more open to share this secret whether the relationship could be saved or not. Whereas two partners who have a pattern of reacting negatively to adverse news and consistently misunderstanding each other may be more reluctant to open up about the transgression.

If your goal is to be an effective communicator and minimize conflict, then you have to identify which obstacles are present within you or your relationship. Whatever that obstacle is, know that you have the ability to fix it and make things better. Even if it requires you to enlist outside help from a professional, another one of our recurring themes.

Communication in Relationships

Hopefully by now you see how communication takes conscious effort. In relationships, the requirement for effort becomes significantly more important because thereare different expectations attached to it. Sometimes it takes effort to ask how someone's day was or even tell them you love them. It takes effort to listen to someone after you've had a long day yourself. But it comes with the territory.

Think of this: how much effort do you exhaust convincing your partner that you are the right one for them? How much time do you spend winning them into your life? How often have you told them that they mean the world to you or anything along those lines? Then how can you not take the time or put in the energy to effectively communicate with them? Earlier we talked about paying attention to perceived communication right. Well, the perceived communication after you've done everything to win their affection and then turn around and not be able to communicate with them is that you really didn't mean all of those things to begin with.

The second strongest form of communication in relationships, next to listening, is action. Action reinforces that you were listening and paying attention when it comes to your partner, and it confirms that you mean what you say when it comes to self. Not only that, but action requires energy whether what you do is for the good or for the bad. That's why when you do something good, it is associated with the effort you put in, and it becomes something special. However, when you do something bad, you still had to put some effort into it and that's what makes it heartbreaking. It's the fact that you chose to put energy into an action that you know would not be in the best interest of your partner. No matter what excuse you use, that's the simple truth of it.

So, if you always act in your partner's best interest, most conversations will be easier to have. That's because you exude a certain level of authenticity when you have nothing to hide, and words tend to become firmer when backed up by action. Action is also one of the first forms of communication to go when complacency starts to set in. Some people start to feel that as time passes they don't have to do as much. Saying "I love you" is relatively easy when compared to finding new ways to show it and maintaining consistency with it. Eventually, without action, those words will become empty.

Another thing to be aware of when communicating in terms of relationships is to, again, stay cognizant that we are all different. Getting into a relationship doesn't take away someone's individuality. But the more comfortable you get with someone, it seems a point comes where you forget how different you both are. In these instances, it becomes much easier to only focus on the ways you are alike. But in doing so, you inadvertently start expecting your partner to communicate the way you would. Ask yourself this: Have you ever been talking to someone and thought, *Why didn't you just say it like this? Or, if I were you, then I would've just said it like that.*

That's you imposing who you are and your interpretations on the other person. You're letting your familiarity with them remove their individuality and expecting responses based on your communication style. The longer you are with someone, there may be areas that you do become similar in, but don't let that detract you from the fact that differences still remain as well. One obvious issue this can create, if someone isn't responding the way you want or expect them to, is you may assume that they are being dishonest or hiding something. And approaching someone with that energy, especially when it's unwarranted, can create tension.

T.A.L.K. It Out

There are so many communication barriers that can lead to conflict that's it's impossible to think you can avoid it altogether. And since you can't avoid it, the best thing to do is plan for it and manage it. With everything we've covered so far, from diversity and emotions to obstacles, the reality of this should be apparent. Below is a tool that I created that has helped me tremendously in communicating with people. I call it T.A.L.K. And like any other tool, it's only relevant if you decide to use it.

Step	Explanation
T: timeout	Take a second to collect yourself and your thoughts, and balance your emotions.
A: assess	Assess all the factors surrounding the conversation. Be present and aware.
L: listen	Listen with the goal of being empathetic and to understand from their POV.
K: keep the focus	Keep the focus on the situation at hand. Don't deflect or bring up the past.

Timeout – This step is used to help manage the human condition, or more effectively, our ability to be emotional and irrational. When you feel yourself getting to the point of being highly emotionally charged, force yourself to take a step back. Don't let the throttle stay on 100, possibly causing things to escalate too far out of hand. To pump the breaks when you are immersed with an emotion is not easy. It will take practice and discipline, but the benefits will be worth it.

This gives you an opportunity to collect your thoughts and balance your emotions—two things that allow you to effectively communicate what you mean to say. Without doing this, you leave yourself open to speak out of frustration and risk, having your pointlost in translation. You can even implement this step before a conversation takes place if you know it will be a sensitive topic. A timeout is for YOU.

Assess – This step is used to help add overall understanding to why the conversation is taking place. You want to assess the mood, the nature of the conversation, what perceptions could be in place, the history with topics like this, and any other relevant factors surrounding the need for the conversation. Taking all of these things into account helps you zero in on the other person's aspect and allows you to get to a place of empathy for what they may be feeling.

Going into a conversationwithout taking a momentto assess these things, you leave yourself open to be caught off guard and therefore can become reactive instead of receptive to what someone is trying to communicate to you. This step is the difference between being pushed and pulled by a conversation versus going into it with a sense of understanding and preparedness. Assessing is for the CIRCUMSTANCES.

Listen – This step is used to help gain perspective. It's also where you can affirm any conclusions made in step two. It requires that you listen empathetically. Not to be judgmental, defensive, passive, or looking for a rebuttal. You have to understand that this person feels the way they do for a reason. And whether you agree with it or not, listening is how you find out why.

To do this effectively requires patience and discipline, but it can be a little easier if you successfully complete the first two steps. You have to empathetically listen even if the delivery isn't to your liking. The first thing most people do when the delivery isn't "likable" (i.e., hot, hostile, angry, etc.) is get defensive or match energies. But by doing this, you actually miss the opportunity to resolve the underlying issue, which could've been something as simple as a misunderstanding. After the issue is resolved, then you can address the delivery method, but handle one fire at a time, which leads us to the next point. Listening is for the OTHER PARTY.

Keep the focus – This step is used to prevent adding fuel to the fire and to create a direct avenue for resolution. When someone brings a problem to you for discussion, that is not the time to meet that problem with another problem, especially one from the past. That is not the time to point the finger and let them know where they've also been wrong. Keep the focus on the issue at hand.

By bringing up past issues or meeting a problem with another problem, you are telling the person you are communicating with that their feelings aren't validated and that they don't deserve to feel the way they do. You put the conversation in a place of tit for tat and only add fuel to the fire as more and more issues start coming up. The pathway to a resolution becomes smaller and smaller until it vanishes. If you do have genuine grievances, then bring them up when they first occur, not as a response to you being in the hot seat. Discuss it, resolve it, and bury it. When you listen empathetically to someone's concerns and keep the focus there, you can then demand that same respect when something arises that you want to discuss. This step is for the RESOLUTION.

If both people communicating agree to use this tool, the amount of truly resolved conflicts will increase significantly. Let's look at a scenario together to see how it looks.

Scenario:

A husband and wife agreed to share the duties of picking the kids up from school. To accomplish this, they assigned themselves designated days. The husband has Tuesday, Thursday, and afterschool activities. The wife has Monday, Wednesday, and Friday. One Thursday, the husband calls the wife around noon and says he won't be able to make it to the kids due to a last-minute work assignment. The wife, a week prior, already made plans with some friends who were coming into town to do a day trip. The husband who is well aware of this has to call his wife and relay the information.

Without T.A.L.K.

The husband is frustrated at the last minute change and calls his wife.

> *Husband: Babe, I can't pick up the kids. Something came up at work, so you have to get them.*
> *Wife: Well, you know I have plans for today. Isn't there anything you can do?*
> *Husband: What can I do, something came up. Trust me, I'm just as upset as you are.*
> *Wife: So do I just cancel my plans?*
> *Husband: I don't know, babe. I'm sorry but I have to go.*

In this scenario, the husband is frustrated and his responses stem from that frustration. Even if he did account for the magnitude of the position this puts his wife in, he's not expressing it. This leaves the wife open to conclude that he doesn't care or didn't do anything to even try to save her plans. Another inference could be the notion that he feels his job makes his time more important than hers. Of course, history, personality, and understanding each other plays a role, but that still doesn't remove the frustration from this inconvenience. Now let's look at this scenario using T.A.L.K.

For this breakdown, I'm not going to use a script. I want to run through this process in depth to add more understanding. For the following paragraphs, quotation marks notate direct speech. The parenthesis includes amplifying information, and everything else is scenario related.

The husband gets word that he has a new deadline for a work project, and in order to meet it he has to stay late at his day job to pick up the kids. First, he informs his boss of the situation to request an extension so he can meet his family obligations. (Surprisingly, there are a lot of people who would skip this step or just not think about it. When things come up at work, we automatically assume it trumps everything else or that our bosses wouldn't understand so we don't even bother reasoning with them. We find it easier to negotiate with our partners to their inconvenience than to confront our employers. Instead of assuming, you have to at least try to make sure you are covering all your bases. Who knows, by simply communicating your concern, it may actually work more times than you think. Also, a "no" in one circumstance doesn't automatically mean there will be a "no" in another. Speak up.) The boss is receiving pressure from higher-ups and can't extend the deadline.

The next thing he should do is try utilizing outside resources by calling his local family members to see if anyone is available to help. Unfortunately, no one can come to his aid this time. (Even though it didn't work, this kind of effort is a testament to how much the husband values his wife and her time. All of this is to make sure before you have that other conversation you've exhausted all other resources. Once you've established that's the type of person you are, it will build character credit with your partner in the future. They'll know that in situations like this, if you have to call them, it's because you tried everything else and nothing came through.) Now it's time to make the call.

The two paragraphs above are a result of taking a timeout and assessing the situation. He's now done everything he can up to this point and can call his wife with honest and confident sincerity for having to interrupt her plans, as well as be ready to receive any reaction given. When making this call, the best thing to do is be straightforward. Now is not the time to beat around the bush, try to sugarcoat it, or manipulate the information. Be confident in the effort you put in beforehand.

Approach it along the lines of, "Babe, I know you have plans with your friends that you made last week, and today is my day to pick up the kids." (This shows you understand the situation and recognize the inconvenience.) "However, something came up at work, and I won't be able to get there in time. I've explained to my boss the situation and called all of our local relatives to see if there was anything else that could be done; nothing came through." (This re-emphasizes the effort you took not to inconvenience her). "Is there anything or other resources on your end we could use in this situation?" (Continued effort and empathy). Next, you listen.

Best case scenario, nothing comes of it, and she just goes to pick them up or has a resource that can help pick up the slack. But still be willing to make it up! Worst case scenario, she vents heavily and you let her. This isn't the time to bring up past scenarios where you had to be the one picking up the slack. Keep the focus on the situation at hand.

Here's where the human factor can make it a bit more complicatedthanitneedstobe. Ofcourse, weallknowthat work is important. And of course, we don't want anyone to get fired or create a negative image of themselves that would be detrimental to professional growth (i.e., always leaving when things are in a crunch). Of course, we know that this is outside of the husband's control. With these three perspectives, especially the one on control, some people would find it very hard to empathize and they would just figure their partner should understand.

That's why it takes strength and maturity to accept responsibility in this type of situation. It's not really about those things. It's about showing compassion and understanding that regardless of how it happened, it happened, and on your watch. "It's not my fault!", "What was I supposed to do?" Responses like that require zero effort, show zero empathy, and have the chance to further undervalue your partner's feelings. Can you see the clear difference?

Try this next scenario on your own. See how you would implement the T.A.L.K. tool. Feel free to email your conclusions to info@qmcdonald.com.

Scenario 2:

A young man and woman have been dating for a few months. He's ready to take things to the next level and asks to meet her family. Since she's already met his family, he thinks it shouldn't be a big deal. But every time he asks to meet them, he's faced with some type of resistance. They've continued to get closer and closer, but there doesn't seem to be an avenue to meet her family anytime soon. He thinks she may be hiding something and wants to have a conversation to see why she won't let him meet her family.

Chapter 5

Dating: Easy or Hard, You Decide

"Sometimes we create our own
heartbreaks through expectation."
~ Anonymous

"If you don't date with a purpose, then
your purpose is solely to date."
~ Quinton D. McDonald

From my junior year in high school through the bulk of my college days, I was what you would consider a "skirt-chaser." But I was never the type to just straight out say, "Can we bone?" I was into the whole wine, dine, and gentleman culture of being intimate with someone. With that being said, I went on a lot of dates... A LOT! I've seen the good, the bad, and the ugly when it comes to getting to know someone. What that enabled me to do is gain great insight into the world of dating and the different mentalities attached to it.

If you are in the dating arena or getting ready to enter it, hopefully you are doing so being truly ready to bring someone into your world. Meaning you have worked on yourself, addressed deficiencies, are comfortable being single, can communicate effectively, and know what you want. These are important to have done because they give you an understanding of what you want/need, and can help you control the pace of your dating phase.

Worst Date Ever

I didn't enter the dating world on that footing. By aimlessly going about it, I got involved with some interesting people, one of which would become the worst date I'd been on in my entire life. I was living in the Washington, D.C. area, and I met a young lady on Tinder. We talked for a few days then decided to meet up. We went to a bar, had some drinks, some laughs, and generally a really good time. She ended up coming back to my house, and though we didn't have sex, we cuddled up and engaged in a nice conversation.

The next day, I had a military function to attend that required I wear my dress uniform. It was a friends and family affair, and she asked if she could come since she had never been to an event like that. With me being super spontaneous and thinking about getting "lucky" if we spent more time together, I decided why not. While there, she was very cordial and conversational, and people were really taking a shine to her. I thought this could be the beginning of something special.

Now the ride back is when things started to get interesting. First, she started showing signs of agitation because we ran into some heavy traffic. She kept repeating the sentences, "Let's just pull over" and "I need a drink." I told her the traffic was just due to an accident, and pulling over would get us back later than if we just stayed with it. I also made a deal to stop at this sports bar I knew of when we got back so we could grab a drink after my haircut appointment.

Fast forward to the good stuff. When we walked into the sports bar and got to the bartender, she ordered us both two drinks which she insisted we chug. Then a third drink just to have. I asked her if she'd like to play some pool, but she said she wasn't any good at it, but she'd watch me play someone else. I saw this older gentleman at a table by himself, so I asked if he'd like to play a couple games. I made sure to keep engaging with her, but after the first game she took off back to the bartender.

She ordered a fourth drink then proceeded to walk around the bar and speak to every guy she saw. I don't know what the conversations were, but some of them came to me afterwards and said things along the lines of, "Bro, just so you know, I wasn't talking to her like that. I think she getting kinda tipsy, but no disrespect." Next, she came over and interrupted the game, along with the conversation we were having, and blurted out, "Hey, boyfriend, I want to talk to you."

The man I was playing was in the middle of a sentence telling me one of his stories from service (he was a veteran, and I was in uniform), so I informed her that was rude. In a kind manner, he said to her, "Don't worry, I'm almost finished." She said, "HE'S MY BOYFRIEND, AND I CAN TALK TO HIM WHENEVER I WANT." I reminded her that we just met, I wasn't her boyfriend, and that she was being really extra and disrespectful. After that, she disappeared back into the crowd talking to guys and got more drinks from the bar.

By this time, I was getting past ready to leave, but she said she didn't want to leave because she was having fun. She even told me that I catfished her because in my profile I made it seem like I was fun, but here I was being a "killjoy." I told her that her behavior was making me not want to have fun. She told me I could leave but she was going to stay. Part of me wanted to sprint, but the other part felt responsible. I brought her there and she was getting drunk, and if something would've happened to her, I would've felt guilty. So I paid our over 200-dollar tab (mostly her drinks) and sat at the corner of the bar waiting for her to be done.

A group of girls walked in and she ended up linking with them. She told them I was her boyfriend and that I had an attitude because she was being a social butterfly. She asked them to inform me that she was a butterfly and I have to let her fly, which they did (LOL). They said, "Come on, let her fly." She asked if I was happy now that she was talking to girls. I ignored her and went back and started playing pool with my veteran friend. Twenty minutes later, she came up to me with the craziest request I've ever gotten on a date, let alone the FIRST!

Keep in mind I'm still in my uniform. She came up to me and said, "Hey, boyfriend, can you let me borrow 40 dollars?" I said, "I'm not your boyfriend, and why in the world are you asking me for money at this point?" She said, "You see the bartender, I know him from another bar, and he's going to sell me a little bit of marijuana and cocaine. I just haven't done it in so long, and I really feel like I deserve it. This is my first time having a babysitter in forever (yes, she has kids), and plus I get really horny after I do cocaine." I asked her if she had lost her entire mind and told her that I would never aid in the purchase of illicit drugs, especially not wearing my military uniform!

The urge to walk out surfaced again. See, my initial plan was to have a couple drinks, go home and change, then go to a club to dance the night away. It wasn't to be stuck in a sports bar all night with this craziness. Anywho, ten minutes later she came back and said, "Hey, boyfriend, you'd be really proud of me." At this point, I'm completely checked out and super irritated, so I ignored her. She continued, "I didn't buy cocaine. I only got a little bit of weed. See? Aren't you proud of me?" I just went back to playing pool. Right when I thought things couldn't get any worse, twenty minutes later the girls' bathroom door burst open, and there she was in a full-blown fist fight with one of her newfound friends.

People were looking at me like, get your girl, and I'm reiterating the fact that we just met, and she's not my girl! When the fight calmed down, I asked her what happened. She said, "This bitch can't be asking me for bumps of my drugs and then talking shit about my friends." Now "bump" is usually associated with cocaine, so I made the comment, "Oh, so you lied. You did end up buying cocaine?" She said she had, but only a little.

Now the bartender came over and said, "You guys have to leave, but this tab has to be paid first." Remember I previously paid a tab of more than 200 dollars, and I didn't drink anything after that. Apparently, she was at the bar not only ordering for herself, but for her newfound friends (pre-fight) as well. I refused to pay it, and so did she. The bartender threatened to call the cops, and she still continued to refuse to pay it. The bartender and I both asked why she would be ordering drinks if she couldn't pay for them. The bartender, being frustrated, just asked us to leave the establishment. I felt bad that he was going to have to eat the whole tab worth more than 120 dollars, so I offered the 30 dollars I had in cash on me, but I was not swiping my card again.

When we got outside, she decided she didn't want to get in the car until she fought the girl again. Thankfully, some people she knew just so happened to be passing by and convinced her to get in the car. I wanted them to take her, but their car was full. Smh... On the drive back to her place, she was saying some really crazy and off-the-wall stuff. Some things even incriminating from her past. As soon as I got her home, I made sure she got in the house okay, then I sped off like a bat out of hell. I had just experienced the worst date of my entire life!

I'm sharing this story because it contains a great example of the kind of person you can meet when you aren't dating with a purpose in mind or for the right reasons. This situation occurred after my divorce when I was only dating for sex. I'd like to think if I was dating with the right intentions and had been the person I needed to be, I could'veavoided that night. I'll cover some of the things I wish I would've done before jumping back into the dating world and how doing things I mentioned in the previous chapters all work together to improve the dating experience. For those who do choose to date just for the purposes of having sex, by knowing yourself and what you want, addressing what you've identified as character flaws, and understanding better how to communicate, then even you should still be able to avoid a catastrophe like the one I experienced.

Initial Considerations in Dating

How many times have you heard people say, "Dating is hard," "Where are all the good men/women?", "Why date when I can do bad all by myself?" or any variation of these? How many experiences have you personally had where you got overwhelmed with dating because of all the chaos that can accompany it? When you put these two things together, dating definitely takes on a bad rap. Then add the fact that there seems to be more people out there with ill intentions than those looking for something genuine, and it makes you wonder... who wants to deal with all that? Then, the other side of the equation is that some of those who are looking for something genuine may not possess all the tools they need to make the process successful or worthwhile.

So what do you do? Some believe it's best to just avoid dating and not deal with all the craziness. They want the perfect match to just fall into their lives serendipitously. Others believe in lowering expectations to not be disappointed as much. But there are a hopeful few who remain optimistic, believing if they stay the course there is somebody out there for them. Ultimately, there is no easy answer. Dating is complicated. And no matter how many dates you go on, unfortunately, you will still fully never figure it out. Trust me, I know. It's because dating isn't just about you (the only factor you can control); it involves bringing another person (the factor you can't control) into the mix.

Remember everyone is different, and that means that everyone's dating process is going to be a little different. People can go about dating in more ways than there are shades on a color wheel. Just like with communication, you can't expect someone to view or approach dating the same way you would. However, there are a few common elements that should be mutual no matter what your process is. Those elements are patience and time.

Yes, spontaneity, serendipity, and hopeless romanticism have their places, but don't use them as an excuse to follow blind ambition too early on. No matter how great something may seem upfront, with time it can always change. If you've allowed yourself to get too attached at the point of change, you'll be that much more hurt and/or drained on the backend. Or worse, you'll try that much harder to hold on to something that may not even be for you. Think of it like this: taking the appropriate time to go through this process and get it right upfront can save six times as much chaos on the backend.

In the interim, it is very important that you don't neglect the factor that you can control—you. Make sure that you never stop taking opportunities to work on yourself. You never know what mixture of person you will encounter, but the better prepared you are, the more equipped you'll be to handle whatever they may be. Work on your life, your finances, your spirituality, your goals and dreams. Don't worry about timing or when or when you'll meet that special person. The right relationship will appear exactly when it's supposed to.

Place your attention on answering questions like these: What is your purpose for dating? What are you looking for? Why do you want to bring someone into your life? What do you have to offer someone else? Simple questions like these often don't even get asked and without these answers, you are dating blindly. With no clear goal in mind, you are more likely to settle with anyone based on how you feel at that moment. Don't do yourself like that.

Imagine the times—and there will definitely be plenty—where you meet someone who seems to be the perfect fit. They'll have great conversation, good vibes, good energy, attraction, and maybe even a little chemistry. In those instances, it's easy to lose sight of the bigger picture—more affectionately the long-term picture—and be ready to dive in headfirst. But there are two things to keep in mind. One, without setting your standard for dating, what measurement are you using to truly know? And two, everyone is on their best behavior when it's time for the job interview, but how many remain that way after being hired?

All of this points back to time and patience being the most important ingredients in dating. Here are some other things to focus on to help you incorporate these elements without worrying about how much time is passing by:

1) Dating is the discovery stage. It's where you learn about the person who could be your potential mate. To do this successfully requires actually

getting to know them, and that's not something that happens overnight.

2) It's practice to get a feel for what it would be like to be with someone. Make sure to maximize the amount of experiences you have, but don't try to squeeze everything in at once. Try to do things that expose you to different parts of their personality and character.

3) It is the stage that defines what type of relationship you will evolve into. Meaning the habits and behaviors you establish here will become the expectation when things progress. Don't take having the ability to shape your relationship for granted. Put the time and effort into this foundational phase to make sure it's a reflection of what you want. If you don't and things change once a title arises, you also risk changing the dynamics of what you built. That's one of the reasons you hear people saying phrases like, "You aren't the same person I fell in love with."

When you see it written out like this, I'm sure you can agree it seems easy. So why do people make it so hard? Why aren't there more people out there willing to be patient, work on themselves, and allow the right relationship to present itself in due time? Why is there this need to rush or this fear of missing out? To properly answer this question, we have to understand what's happening in the body when we are attracted to or like someone and how it can influence how we feel.

The Mind Plays Tricks

Whenyoufindyourselfattractedtosomeoneorencounter someone that you really like, your body reacts. Whether you notice it or not, you may even get a little excited about it. On a biological level, our physical bodies are primed to have us find someone to mate with. It's self-preservation to form a relationship so that reproduction and continuation of our lineage can occur. The biological level of "love" doesn't care whether the person will be an excellent life-long partner for you; it just wants to bring you together.

So when you meet someone that you are interested in or attracted to, your brain responds by releasing very select chemicals. Chemicals that begin to play tricks on you by interacting with the pleasure center of your brain and influencing your emotions. These chemicals can take things like infatuation, desire, and lust, and make them feel like love and destiny. But how can that be the true feeling of love when you can experience these feelings with multiple people at the same time?

Let's look at three of these chemicals and analyze their effects on the body. After reading, reflect on past circumstances to see if any of this sounds familiar. The first chemical is norepinephrine. This chemical has many functions, but in terms of our topic, it is released as a response to attraction. When present in the body, this chemical can cause your heart rate to increase and decrease your desire to eat and/or sleep. It can enact on many of the reward centers in the brain and make you feel highly alert and energetic... excited!

The second chemical is dopamine. This chemical has the ability to influence motivation and reward goal-directed behavior. You may become more inclined to find ways to please the person responsible for its release. It can make you feel giddy and euphoric and positively influence the things you perceive. Meaning there's a chance that you may become blind to a person's flaws and only focus on the things you want to see in them.

Ask yourself, have you ever had an argument with a close friend or family member because they kept trying to tell you negative things about the person you were dating, but you just couldn't see it? If they truly have your best interest at heart, and considering they aren't being influenced by this chemical like you are, there may be truth to it. In some cases, you may have even found out down the road (post chemicals) how truthful they actually were.

The third chemical I'll mention is serotonin. This one is unique because it's not produced when you are attracted to someone; rather, it is reduced. With normal levels of serotonin, a person can expect to have regulated levels of happiness, satisfaction, and optimism. When these levels drop, people can be more susceptible to behaviors related to Obsessive Compulsive Disorder (OCD) and overthinking. "Why haven't they responded yet!?" And just like norepinephrine, having low levels of serotonin can decrease your appetite and desire to sleep.

Now, those chemicals are produced as a result of being attracted to or infatuated with someone. And as I'm sure you can agree, those effects are already pretty convincing. What happens when you add physicality into the mix? Now you are stimulating the release of a chemical called oxytocin. Oxytocin increases the desire for cuddling and touch. It's also known as the bonding hormone because of how it increases how connected you feel to others. The more you indulge in touching, the more oxytocin is produced. In the beginning of a relationship, having too much oxytocin can once again convince you that you feel something more than is really there.

Keeping in mind everything we just covered so far in terms of what's happening with your body during times of like or attraction, does any of this sound familiar? "I can't stop thinking about you. I don't want to eat. I can't sleep. I just want to talk to/be around you," "Everything about you is amazing. You just make me feel so happy," "I'm willing to do whatever it takes to make this last forever," "Why aren't they responding!?" Have you experienced any of these feelings before and convinced yourself it must be love?

When you see how love is portrayed in movies, music, and books, who wouldn't think they've found it at this point? Unfortunately, much like myself, I'm sure you've also realized that these simulated feelings don't last forever. They fade away as the chemicals dissipate and return to normal levels within the body. At that point, you are faced with the reality of what remains. This transition out of the chemical love phase can be characterized by a few signs, two of which are being easily irritated by things you thought were cute and all of a sudden finding yourself being impatient with things you once were patient with.

If nothing was put into the foundation and you just moved forward based on these false emotions, then you are essentially setting yourself up for failure when it ends. And for those who believed it actually was love, they will experience an actual heartbreak. Our bodies can't differentiate between it being real or not, it's up to you to understand what's going on.

Even though the emotions are chemically driven, there are some people who get addicted to having that initial high. So when one of these relationships ends, they are off to the races to find someone else to give them that feeling again. This scenario plays out way more than it should. And even though it's not recognized by the American Psychiatric Association, many therapists have labeled this as "romance addiction." And it sucks when a person who is just chasing the chemical high encounters someone who genuinely wants to build something meaningful.

Your Past Can Be a Contributing Factor

Just like chemicals can influence how you think you *feel* about a person, there are certain elements of your past (even as far back as childhood) that have the ability to influence the *type* of person you are attracted to. Everything from the morals, beliefs, and patterns you were exposed to, to the types of relationships you've been in up to this point all play a part. To illustrate this, let's start by asking two questions: 1) Did you feel wanted or unwanted as a kid? and 2) What were the common dynamics of the relationships you've been involved in throughout your life?

For question number one, let's first look at growing up in an environmentwhere you felt loved. Under these conditions, there is a higher chance for you to exhibit a boosted self-esteem and have a more solid foundation on what a meaningful relationship should feel like. You more than likely have a positive view of what love is as an emotion, and you can give and receive it easily. These attributes can make it easy for people to gravitate toward you, and by having been positively reaffirmed throughout your life, there wouldn't be a need to rush into discovering these emotions with someone else. They can be patient with the process and wait for it to come along the way they want it to versus looking for it in all the wrong places.

On the other hand, if you grew up feelingunwanted (and everyone can be affected differently), there is a higher chance for you to display one of two primary behaviors. Either 1) not having a proven baseline of what love should be, you may latch on to the substitute feelings of lust, infatuation, or partnership in an attempt to just have something fill that space, or 2) you become skeptical of love, shy from it, and can't readily give or receive it. You may even realize that this route also accompanies trust issues in people. And you typically won't be willing to take the risks involved in forming a genuine relationship, like being vulnerable.

For question number two, what kind of relationships were you exposed to growing up? Were they happy, toxic, dependent, abusive... were you even able to identify what the dynamics were? Even if you don't think that you paid attention to the relationships around you, subconsciously they made an impression. What was the standard in your immediate family? Was positive speech encouraged? Was affection given freely? Was mutual respect consistently practiced? If you grew up under these conditions, more than likely you will seek a partner who possesses those same characteristics.

Unfortunately, for some, this also works in reverse. If you grew up in an environment that was toxic or conflict enriched, you may not even know what a healthy relationship is supposed to be. This means you may gravitate toward what you are familiar with even though it's bad for you. Truly, healthy relationships would feel foreign, and you wouldn't know how to trust them until you unlearn that pattern of thinking.

Unlearning something can be done the same way as learning. Just surround yourself with influences that inspire the thoughts you want to embrace. You are actually doing something right now, in reading this book, that's helping you do this. You can also take courses and/or seek a counselor if you are unable to do it on your own. Another form of influence is to try and identify the healthy couples already around you. Spend time getting familiar with how they operate, communicate, and problem-solve. Eventually, if you dedicate yourself to one or more of these methods, you will notice how the way you think starts to change. You'll notice how you are rewriting that comfort zone of a box you grew up in that was dictating the type of people you let into your life.

The last part of understanding how your past can influence your dating is taking into consideration the beliefs and principles your family practiced. Do you all believe in being tight-knit? Do you believe in gender roles? Do you openly allow in strangers or stay isolated? Again, on a subconscious level, these things have the ability to affect your taste in people. All of this is another reason why it's so important to know yourself. Identify these things so when you start dating, you can recognize the kind of person you may be attracting or attracted to.

From the chemicals in our brain to the things of our past and their ability to influence us, it should be more apparent why taking time with dating is a must. You have to give these things time to work themselves out and get to the root of why you are drawn to a person. Only then, after the noise dies down, can you determine what's causing you to be attracted to them. Even if it is just a chemical attraction or one based on familiarity, understanding it will help give you a sense of direction on how to proceed accordingly.

Single and Ready to Mingle—Online

After my seconddivorce, I reverted back to being a dating connoisseur. I had five different apps downloaded, and I was a swiping machine. I was nowhere near ready to actually date, but I became proficient with the process all the same. For the purpose of this section, lets presume you are ready to date, taking into consideration everything we've covered so far, let's dive into the meeting phase of dating.

Today, there are a ton of options when it comes to meeting people. One of the more popular ways is online dating apps. There is an abundance of dating apps available to choose from and they each offer access to vast dating pools. The convenience of this hand-held speed dating revolution is the primary contributor for more people meeting digitally for the first time than in person. And, regardless of the many horror stories you've heard or even experienced, online dating (when done right) is not bad at all.

As human beings we can only be in one place at a time. What happens if your soulmate is never at the same place at the same time as you? How could you ever meet them? Or maybe you did see them but you were afraid to speak because an opportunity didn't present itself, or you made assumptions like them being already taken. This is where dating apps reign supreme. They give you a broader and longer field of view for who is out there, and not only that, but who is actively looking to date.

The two primary downsides to dating apps for those looking to date seriously anyways are saturation and determining intent. Saturation is where you end up connecting with too many people at the same time. Yes, this is possible as I've seen people with an excess of one hundred people they were matched with. When trying to talk to even half that amount of people, you will find it's practically impossible to engage in meaningful conversations with them all. It gets hard to distinguish one from the other, conversations run together, and some get lost in translation (and they may have been the good ones).

Not to mention it's even harder to narrow down if there is a genuine connection with any one of them. I'm not going to lie—serial swiping can be fun because you never know what you are going to get. But when it comes to actually engaging with them, a suggestion would be to develop a system designed to eliminate those you know "aren't it" upfront. Don't entertain every one of them or give them all the time of day because there will be still be plenty of people who do possess the qualities you seek to sift through. It usually helps to have three to five questions that let you know if someone needs to stay or go. Even then, still try to limit engagements to no more than five people at a time so that you can genuinely interact, differentiate, and actually spend a decent time talking to them before a meet-up.

Trying to determine intent is what decimates online dating. We are all strangers online, and you can't really tell what someone's true intentions are until they choose to reveal them to you. This means you won't be able distinguish right off the bat those who use these apps as intended, to find and build meaningful relationships, from those who only want to find sex partners. If people were honest and upfront, this wouldn't be an issue, but some people can play one role knowing all the while their intentions are the other. If you just want sex, there is nothing wrong with that; just be honest about it even if you don't think it'll lead you to your goal.

It is this type of dishonesty that gives online dating the bad rap. One person is investing in a potential future while the other is only investing to achieve instant gratification, but doing and saying all the right things. This leavespeoplefeeling betrayed and hurt, and now the next person might have to pay for it. When determining someone's intent, you have to ask the right questions and trust your gut as to whether you think the answers are legit. Some may be bold enough to tell you upfront what they really want, but again others like to play the "game." Only time will reveal a person's true intentions. Heck, some people who online-date have whole girlfriends or wives. So again, ask the right questions and trust yourself.

This doesn't just apply to your potential matches, but it applies to you as well. Don't let yourself be the one playing the game. If you know someone is looking for something serious and you aren't, clearly communicate that to them. More people will be okay with this than you'd imagine. And it would be even more enjoyable because you both signed up for it and no one is being lied to or deceived. However, if they aren't feeling it, unmatch them and move on. Don't selfishly string people along just to have options down the road.

Single and Ready to Mingle—In Person

If online dating isn't your thing, don't worry. People still meet the old-fashioned way as well—in person. It's not obsolete, though it is becoming a lost art. It seems the more some people rely on technology, the less efficient we get with communication skills (hence the whole chapter on communication). Before we get into that, meeting people in real life for the first time usually happens one of two ways. The first is serendipitously. Right place, right time, and the right moment presents itself for conversation. Sometimes you have to create that moment, but opportunity is there. This can happen anywhere. Church, grocery store, coffee shop, walking down the street, work, while on vacation... you just look up and there they are.

The downside here is that you just don't know where a person is in life or what they are going through the moment you decide to approach them. There's no posted profile floating above their heads to give any hints or clues, so you are literally taking a chance based off interest and attraction alone. (Side note: That's not to say that people can't lie on profiles and still create this situation of walking in blindly.) You have to be willing to peel the layers back to see who you are dealing with, hence the importance of time and patience.

When approaching someone in person you have to allow that rejection is an option. However, I see a lot of guys getting rejected and getting mad immediately afterwards. Yes, it takes a little bit of courage to approach someone, but that doesn't entitle you to the time or answers you want. Someone who is well-balanced and mature will understand that there is a variety of reasons for being "rejected," most of which have nothing to even do with them. But these men get into their feelings so fast they don't even consider anything outside of it being an act of disrespect. If you are one of those men reading this and can admit it, then my brothers, these next few paragraphs are for you.

Note for my fellas

Just because a woman says she's not interested doesn't mean there is something wrong with you. Consider these scenarios: Maybe she just got fired from her job and doesn't feel like talking to anyone. Maybe she is in a relationship already. Maybe she just broke up with her boyfriend and doesn't want to entertain anyone right now. Maybe she got bad news about a family member who is about to die, and she's too worried about that to engage in a genuine conversation. Maybe she has kids and, out of concern for their safety, doesn't take lightly to strangers. Maybe she's in a rush to get somewhere and she's already late, so she just has to keep it moving. Maybe she's on her period, not feeling well, has to go to the bathroom, etc. Also keep in mind she's not obligated to share any of this information with you.

Maybe, she gets approached by 10 different guys a day, and they all do the exact same thing. Show interest at first but as soon as she doesn't respond the way they want her to, they get an attitude or become disrespectful. Maybe she's tired of that cycle and wants someone mature enough to accept and understand her not being available to talk right then. Maybe she wants to see if you are willing to put in consistent effort (playing hard to get) instead of being a man who simply wants immediate gratification.

There are literally hundreds of reasons why she may not want to talk to you at that exact moment and only one of them deals with you. Which means yes, we also have to admit the fact that she just may not be into you for whatever reason. Everyone does not have to like you because you like them. Get over yourself and respect her not wanting to be bothered or talked to. One thing for certain is that if you do give her a negative response, she was right about choosing not to give you the time of day because your interest wasn't real.

A suggestion would be when you approach someone, do it respectfully. If that person doesn't show interest, be genuine in apologizing for interrupting their day, accept it for what it is with maturity and respect, and wish them well for the rest of the day. That's called planting seeds. She may not have been in the mood to talk at that moment, but if her situation changes and an opportunity presents itself again, she'll remember those who were respectful. And next time you see her, still be polite and speak. Don't ignore her or assume she's a "certain way" because of her head space the last time you encountered her. She may surprise you.

I want to point back to consistent effort. What if she actually does get approached by ten different guys a day? What is going to set you apart? What is going to differentiate your approach from the rest of the bunch? If you are genuinely interested in pursuing something with her and not just showing fake interest like the rest to accomplish some short-term goal, then put some effort into your approach. If she's not in the mood today, show consistency and try again the next time you see her. But use judgment and pay attention because sometimes a no is just that—a no. Don't push too hard or too far and end up getting yourself branded as a creeper.

Just show that you want more than a quick acknowledgment and you are willing to be patient and earn it. If you can't do that in the beginning to get her, what message are you sending about what it would be like to be in a relationship with you?

Note for women

For your role in this, please understand that there is a thin line between playing hard to get to make sure someone really likes you and stringing someone along selfishly. Also, in today's society, you don't have to be afraid to take your shot if there is someone that you like. Nobody wants to face potential rejection, but sometimes it helps to put yourself out there. Part of being comfortable with yourself is understanding that a no isn't the end of the world. That just wasn't the person for you, but at least you were courageous enough to find out.

Communication is a two-way street; and words definitely matter. So make sure the things you communicate verbally and non-verbally align with what you really want, with who you really want, and who you really are. Just like you don't want a man to play games with you, don't be the one playing games with him.

SingleandReadytoMingle—InPerson(Cont'd)

The second way people meet in person is through events/ activities. This is when you go somewhere for the specific purpose of meeting people to potentially date. These places include bars, clubs, speed dating, mixers, blind dates, and any other arena with the ultimate purpose of bringing singles together. This method definitely eases some pressure because like with dating apps, you know that for the most part other people there have the same goal in mind. It's just a matter of finding people out of the crowd you vibe the most with. In these instances, you also get that in-person interaction to get a better feel of who and how they are before agreeing to go on a one-on-one date.

The potential downside to this is since it's planned, peoplehave time to preparethe best version of themselves or,as we discussed earlier, put on theirmasks. This means that although you get to see them, you may be observing their interview face. But interview face or not, if you feel good vibes, you feel good vibes. Don't overthink it or ignore that. Rather, use caution in proceeding forward so time has a chance to weed the bad ones out. Until then, live in the moment, enjoy yourself, and have fun. As you mingle through the crowds, keep in mind your primary purpose for being there and the expectations you set for the type of person you want. These events can't last forever, and doing this will make sure you don't waste too much time entertaining the wrong people.

What Lies Beneath the Mask?

Whether you prefer online or in person, when it comes to meeting people, be your most true and authentic self. I can't express that enough. Eventually, they will meet the real you and it is better to introduce your real self earlier than later. If you are concerned that the real you isn't a catch or will scare someone away... then are you really ready? Be honest with yourself and the person you are dating. Don't portray a character that's a completely different version of your true self. Be aware; masks come in different varieties. You have personality masks, character masks, circumstance masks, financial masks, moral masks, etc. They all do the same thing: hide your true nature to draw others near.

But masks are temporary. Portraying something that you're not takes effort, and effort takes energy. Eventually, a person will run out of energy and start revealing who they really are. This is not a new concept, but the problem comes in when people move so fast that they are in "love" before the mask has even had a chance to budge. You can't accuse someone of changing it up on you when you didn't really know who they were to begin with. Instead of going around and asking why people can't just be real, recognize that another question is, why can't you give them the time to be?

By wearing these facades, some people have become accustomed to telling others what they want to hear instead of delivering straightforward truths. Collectively, we must break this trend. Yes, at times the truth can be a little uncomfortable or a bit much, which can make it hard to deliver and hard to receive. But so what? That momentary discomfort of being seen as mean, inconsiderate, or as a jerk is nothing compared to what can happen if the lie plays out instead. Hurt feelings heal over time, but you never get wasted time back.

Masks don't just affect what you put out, but they can impact what you accept too. So when you start accepting or allowing things to transpire that you know you wouldn't be alright with in the long term, you are setting yourself up. This goes back to dating being the phase that determines what type of relationship you'll evolve into. If there are things you don't like, address them early. And since people are ever evolving, if something changes in how you feel as things progress, again, address it. Don't let your mask make youpassive just to keep someone's attention/affection.

In general, you should never feel like you have to coddle someone's needs or emotions or play down or up to their egos. It's not your job to ease someone else's insecurities or emotional instability at this stage no matter how much you like them. And don't let them make you feel guilty for not doing so either. Be true to yourself and everything will work out in the end. That's not saying dump everything out at once, but it is saying put those important things on the forefront before things progress past a certain point.

Be confident enough in who you are and what it is that you want that you don't have to be inauthentic. Also, be able to communicate those things clearly. Don't be afraid to have those sensitive conversations or discover/reveal sensitive information because you fear that it may cause things not to work out. If it's a part of who you are now, then it will always be a part of your story. Eventually, it will come out. If it's something that bad, where you have to contemplate sharing it, then know that trying to pad the surface with all of your "good" qualities first won't make the information less impactful. All in all, just be real!

What Are We Looking For?

Now that you've met some seemingly interesting people online or in person, the next step is getting to know them. The purpose of getting to know someone is to determine if there is long-term compatibility and to establish a baseline of comfortability. Compatibility is the one that most people focus on but being comfortable with someone is equally important. That's the one that's going to take the most time to establish because it involves trust.

Your best friend wasn't your best friend overnight. You had to get to a point of being comfortable with them, which entails establishing a certain level of familiarity and trust in them. You can see compatibility from the surface level sometimes, but comfort is built through time and proven action. Keep in mind that it is definitely possible to have one without the other, as they are not mutually exclusive.

Let's look deeper into what these two words mean. Oftentimes when it comes to dating (or relationships), words are just thrown around because they sound good, but there is no depth of understanding as to what they actually imply. Words like compromise, compassion, empathy, selflessness, and love are all examples of words that people can use without truly understanding the meaning behind them.

For compatibility, it's how well two things can go together without having adverse reactions or conflict. If two things are extremely compatible, they will mesh together, requiring little to no force and causing little to no adverse reactions. As the level of compatibility decreases between two things, the amount of force required to make them fit will increase proportionally, and the reactions become more negative as well. In people this can be reflected in anything, from the differences of values, beliefs, morals, culture, heritage, and mindset to personality traits, intellect, aspirations/goals, and/or perspectives.

There are a number of factors that can contribute to how well two people fit together or how volatile they are together. We've all heard the saying "opposites attract," so being "zero resistance" compatible with someone is very rare. You probably wouldn't want that anyways because let's face it, having some difference makes things more interesting. Most people don't want to date someone exactly like them. Just like we talked about in the chapter on communication, difference yields better results when it comes to areas like planning and collaboration.

The intent should be to find someone that requires a minimal amount of resistance to be with. Someone with just enough difference to make it exciting but not enough that every day is a fight. You can pick up hints on how compatible you are with a person if you really listen to them when they speak. Between that and what they show you through action, use your gut and trust your instincts to determine how well you mesh with someone. Something to be aware of... there are people who are willing to trade levels of compatibility to gain things that are pleasant to have. For instance, accepting a low-compatibility or high-resistance relationship just to be with someone because they look good or have a lot of money. Our society as a whole places great emphasis on theseattributes, makingthemhighlysoughtoutovermore important things like peace of mind. Sometimes people will even choose having one of these over happiness. If you really are at a point in your life that you want the real thing, don't be willing to trade the important things for things that ultimately won't affect your inner peace.

Comfortability is getting to a point where you trust someone enough to be completely transparent and vulnerable with them. Whether that's sharing sensitive information or trusting them enough to make decisions that will affect your life, you have minimal to no reservations. When I say sensitive information, Imean anything that could make you susceptible to any kind of harm or misfortune if misused. And the decisions can range from things like allowing someone to meet people closest to you (family, children, best friends) to things like deciding where you'll live, where you'll vacation, what type of lifestyle you'll lead, etc.

When you put it like that, then even the most spontaneous person should use caution getting to this point. Yet you see it in movies, and emulated in real life, all the time where things move too fast. Because things seem so great in the beginning, the relationship progresses to a point beyond what the individual was actually ready for. They start allowing certain privileges and accesses only to end up regretting it down the road.

Don't let anyone force you into a level of comfort you aren't ready for. If they can't give you the requisite time to get there naturally, you may want to question their motives and/or assess if that's really the person for you.

So as you are getting to know someone for who they are, also ask yourself these questions: Would you trust this person with your secrets or your body? Would you trust them with your family or with your finances? Would you trust that they will always act in your best interest? Questions that only time, along with a history of proven actions, should suffice in answering. If you can't say with great confidence, "I am comfortable enough to trust this person with multiple aspects of my life," then act accordingly, and don't let the courtship (relationship) advance past certain levels.

Don't allow yourself to get put into predicaments to have to make those types of premature decisions under any circumstances. It can be easier said than done because in the heat of the moment, those human elements we discussed earlier can take over. However, just remaining conscious of this should help you manage effectively.

Other Factors to Consider

Compatibility and comfortability are big things to look for, but what else are we looking for in the initial phases of dating?

There's a judgment of attraction. If you met someone online, the first thought is usually if they really look like their pictures. Even with video chatting being available, camera magic and catfishing are real things. Many people want to put their best "face" forward when it comes to dating, so it's very rare that you'll see a profile with someone using no cosmetics, filters, or angles. Unfortunately, our society places so much emphasis on a specific type of beauty that a lot of people actually think they need those extra touches just to get attention. And sadly, sometimes they are right.

Now, let me be fair and point out that, yes, there is nothing wrong with cosmetics, however, there is a distinct difference between touch-ups and re-creation. Wearing a physical mask can be just as deceitful as wearing a metaphorical one. And if your goal is to progress with someone, eventually they will see the real you. If your before and after images are night and day, you have to be willing to accept whatever the outcomes may be. If yourthought process isusing enhanced beauty features to draw someone close, hoping your personality will win them over in the end, you have to expect it may not work out that way as well.

The more transparent and honest you are in what you look like, the more it prevents people from feeling lied to later on. That goes for men and women. I've heard several stories of guys who were four feet nothing and that fact wasn't revealed until the actual date. Again, not an issue, but height is something many people consider. The bottom line though is when you find your person, they will find you attractive no matter what. If you think you have to do extra for someone to find you attractive, they may not be the one.

Also, understand that attraction is built on multiple characteristics, including but not limited to height, weight, facial features/symmetry, rhythm of walk, style of dress, hair, manner of speech, voice, personality, and level of confidence or success. With that being said, the same rules for appearance apply to people presenting themselves as something they are not (the metaphorical mask). Like the people who took their stimulus money (since this is a thing now), tax refunds, or financial aid money and pretended to be a baller. They know good and well they can't maintain that level of living, but they definitely put on a full stunt.

This, again, is why it is very important to be your true and authentic self. Don't put out an artificial persona of yourself to draw someone in, hoping that personality and charm will win them over in the end. The aftermath is not worth it, trust me. This is me speaking from an abundance of experience with doing this. Because when it comes out that you aren't who you pretended to be, you never know how a person will respond to that display of selfishness.

There's a feel for chemistry. Plain and simple: "Do we vibe?" Do we find each other likeable, and is there a genuine connection between us? Sometimes you can feel this on a first date, but other times it may take a few dates for it to click (if at all). Chemistry is one of those building blocks essential to having romance in relationships. Think of this: You can find ways in which you are compatible with a complete stranger if you look for them. And you might have some really good friends whom you are comfortable with, but you'd still never date. This is the magic of chemistry, more specifically sexual chemistry. It's the difference between platonic and romantic.

Two things to be cautious of are: 1) Chemistry can be felt differently through different means (i.e., phone calls and messaging versus in person). 2) Chemistry can be one-sided.

Have you ever been speaking with someone on the phone and felt there was a strong connection, but in person that feeling just doesn't seem to resurface? Or have you ever misread a situation to think that you were on the same page with someone else only to find out you were by yourself? To fully understand if chemistry is present and how potent it is, just pay close attention, communicate clearly, and trust yourself.

There are many things that people can look for when dating, but these two hereare the primary reasonspeople jump into relationships prematurely. For instance, you meet someone, you are really attracted to them, there seems to be a shared sense of chemistry, things are going great so far on the date, and conversation is flowing. At this point, some may be ready to take things up a notch. In this kind of situation, everything we've covered so far as it relates to dating just seems to go out the window. Instead of thinking logically to understand why you feel certain things, you just succumb to the emotional avalanche, and the rest... will be history.

If things truly are going that great, then the only thing you've proven so far is that potential exists. Don't ignore it but don't pull the trigger too quickly either. Look to see if it's consistent and if it's evolving. If the first dates are the plateau, then what else do you have to look forward to? Nothing is wrong with wanting to dig deeper with someone if you feel something special, but understand that wanting a relationship too early on could be attributed to any of the things we mentioned earlier, neither of which was true love. Plus, if this is the person you are destined to be with, then it doesn't matter how long it takes (within reason) to have a title because you will still be together regardless.

Exercising patience and restraint is especially important if either of the following or similar scenarios apply to you: a) if you're tired of being single, b) if you've recently gotten out of a relationship, c) if all your friends are getting married and/or having babies and you feel behind the curve, d) if you are getting tired of the dating scene and just want someone good enough, and e) someone came along who is better than what you've been getting.

Circumstances like these can cause you to make decisions hastier than you normally would and potentially cause you to lower your standards. In order to avoid succumbing to those thoughts, make yourself recognize if conditions like these or similar ones exist in your life. Then take a second to really see if they could be impacting how you feel. Hold on to the idea that dating is a process and rushing for any reason can be a recipe for disaster. Continue getting to know each other and in time, you'll be able to realize if those initial thoughts or emotions were real or not. Patience really is a virtue.

You Aren't Committed Until You Are Committed

Okay, apparently, I have to say this. The purpose of dating is to find the person you want to commit to. Don't treat people like they are obligated to do or say anything at this point because truthfully they're not. Even if they schedule a date with you and decide not to show up, that's their prerogative. Now, for common decency, at least a phone call should be made so you aren't wasting anyone's time. But if a person isn't that considerate, it shows you who they are. Cut your losses and move on. Don't dwell on feeling owed something.

The best way to go into dating is with the understanding that nothing is owed to you and at this point, you are both only agreeing to get to know each other. Live in the moment because of all the prospects a person could have, you are the ones in front of each other right now. Instead of putting focus on what should happen or what you want to happen, put effort into giving them reasons to see you again. Don't bog a person down with expectations too early on. This shows maturity and understanding and allows you to just appreciate the moments, while in the meantime you are letting things progress naturally. Take it one date at a time.

What can happen is one person starts feeling the other way too fast, and they start putting expectations in place. Like, I have to talk to you this many times, see you this many times, go out however so often, and let's cut everyone else off and only talk to each other. These conditions can be a sign of insecurity. People only try to put these types of measures in place when they don't want to lose the person in front of them, but it can also come off as desperation and push someone away. Not only that, but being insecure is one of the signs a person may not be ready for something serious because remember you should be comfortable with yourself first.

If you know your value and what you have to offer, then when the right person comes along they'll see it too. They won't have to be pressured into spending more time with you. So if you find yourself getting into situations where you continuously feel you are giving more than the other person, you may want to check your pace. A repeated theme, and I'm going to say it again, don't rush this process! Slow down, and shift gears. Even if that means going back and focusing solely on you.

Think about this: You may not even be the only one this person is dating, but because you want to move fast and implement protective measures, you just sabotage your chances of going further with them. Speaking of which, this is another place where open and honest communicationisnecessary. Wheresomepeoplemayonly date one person at a time, there are those who believe it's necessary to date multiple people at a time. Neither way is right or wrong, but intentions should be understood. Again, this is more of a common decency measure that is helpful in preventing people from developing their own ideas or risking playing with someone's emotions.

Now, if you did verbally agree to exclusively date, then that's different. In that scenario, you can have a minimum expectation for the person you made the agreement with to honor the terms of it. However, it should be understood that without a title it can change at any moment. That doesn't mean you should try to force it or rush a title. The pursuit of a title can actually detract you from getting to know a person, which is where your focus should be. Find out who the person you are dating is. Discovery conversations shouldnever stop in the beginning. I've seen some relationships get stagnant really fast because they "run out of things to talk about." If it stops progressing or doesn't seem to be building to anything, consider what you are doing.

Yes, it is okay to walk away from a situation if it's not to your liking. There is no commitment! Don't feel obligated to stay where you aren't growing, progressing, or happy. Many of us have to get better at this. I know it can be uncomfortable and you may feel a certain degree of responsibility to their feelings (depending on how long you have been talking), but that's part of adulting. You have to make the hard choices that lead to better outcomes for your life down the road.

Things that can increase the difficulty of letting go are accepting way more than is given. You know those people who come out the gate on full throttle doing any and everything for the person they are dating. Expensive gifts, out-of-town trips, etc. They say it ain't tricking if you got it, but trust me, those higher-level gifts come with expectations. If youare uncertain if a person is right for you, then realize you don't have to accept everything. Don't let those things be a factor in your consideration to leave or stay because now you have to worry about being perceived as a user. You aren't committed until you are, so in all areas, to keep confusion from entering the picture, just act according to that philosophy.

Sex—The Incapacitator

Lastly, when it comes to dating, if your goal is to find someone to be serious with, don't rush into having sex too soon! I've heard people use the expression, "You gotta have a 'test drive'" as justification when really it doesn't need to be justified. People just like having sex, which is another reason why having self-discipline is extremely important. Remember the chemical oxytocin, notably the most powerful influencer your brain can produce, is released in response to physical touch. So you may be purposely persuading yourself to favor a person who could be toxic all because the sex is good.

I can personally vouch for the importance of being sexually satisfied in healthy relationships. However, like everything else we've covered so far, getting to sex is a process and it should take time. The benefits of allotting that time is extreme. You forgo influencing your natural thoughts about a person, you forgo creating a false notion as to how you feel about someone, you avoid the risk of disease or premature pregnancy, you avoid having your energy tied to a person who could be no good for you, and you can focus on other aspects of really getting to know someone without being motivated by trying to get to physicality.

Additionally, for people who are only motivated by the flesh, there is no quicker way to reveal their true intent than by making them wait. On the other hand, there is no quicker way to see if a person truly values you for you than someone who is willing to wait. Never feel pressured to take that step no matter how great someone appears. You'd be surprised at how incredible someone can "act" when they want to accomplish certain goals.

Some of you have experienced this and yet keep falling for it.

I'd hate to be the bearer of bad news, but if you feel that intimacy is the only way to keep a person's interest, you may want to reevaluate your self-esteem or what qualities you truly possess. Male or female, know this: You are a prize and the only person/people who should have access to that prize are those who are truly worth it. When it's truly right, beyond all doubt, you'll know. Trust your instincts.

Listed below are some additional discovery questions you can ask during the dating phase to gauge a person's character. These just serve as guidelines. You are free to develop your own list based on what's important to you. Also, if done right some of these questions can be asked before a face-to-face meet-up ever occurs as sort of a weeding out process. I'd recommend that you identify things that are definite deal breakers. Include them in the initial conversations prior to one-on-one to save you and them some time.

- Are you truly single or is there anyone who believes they are in a relationship with you?
- Do you have any ties to past relationships like having kids or being legally separated and not divorced?
- What's important to you at this stage in your life?
- How do you prioritize things in your life?

- What belief system do you belong to?
- Where's one place that you've never been to that you've always wanted to visit?
- Do you set goals? What is the next goal on your list to accomplish?
- What are some of your interests, hobbies, and/or skill sets?
- How would you feel about dating someone who wants to wait until marriage to have sex?
- How would being in a relationship right now add to your life or the goals you've set?

Chapter 6

Considerations for Relationships

*"A successful marriage requires falling in love
many times, always with the same person."*
~ Mignon McLaughlin

I naperfectworld,everyonewouldbethemostcomplete
and authentic versions of themselves. We would have
our affairs in order, and we would date with a defined
purpose in mind. We'd seek meaningful and fulfilling
relationships and we'd have the tools to make them last.
We'd take our time getting to know each other and be
patient as the process unfolds into something beautiful.
Unfortunately, grand scale, we live in a world that is less
than perfect. So what we see instead are people who
are broken, lost, damaged, confused, and/or immature
jumping into relationships.

It wouldn't be that badif peopleactually learned from
the mistakes they made. But based on my experience,

there are too many people who don't do that or even have the ability to recognize what their mistakes are. They shy away from taking responsibility for their actions and behaviors, and just hope the next person can deal with their issues better. But isn't that the same definition as insanity? Doing the same thing over and over expecting different results? As I mentioned in the introduction, if you want to have more fulfilling relationships, then you have to consider doing things in ways you haven't been doing them before.

And it starts with the self. If you are considering a relationship with someone, hopefully you are ready to embark on this journey. Know that it will not be easy, but by developing attributes within yourself such as patience, humility, selflessness, communication, empathy, and discipline (most of which we've talked about so far), it can be a lot less difficult. Remember, it's not about being perfect; it's about having an understanding of what is required to be in a successful relationship and having the tools and discipline to do it more times than not. And if you and your partner are both willing to put in that type of conscious effort daily, you can have a top-tier relationship.

Going back to Chapter 3, if you know you are not prepared, then don't jump into a relationship trying to figure it out along the way. There will be plenty of challenges inherently in a relationship that won't benefit from the compounding of your internal stuff.

Don't try to slay two dragons at the same time. Address one before confronting the other, and address the one that presents the most immediate threat: yourself. Leaving this dragon undefeated will almost always contribute to your relationship unraveling before it can even begin.

And just to put this out there, please do not try to use a new relationship as a Band-Aid for the last one. There's a saying that goes, "Hurt people hurt people." Your emotional scars can affect the person you are with, causing them to affect the next person they are with. And as this process goes on and on, can you see the type of cycle it creates?

What is a relationship though? Defined, it's the way in which two or more people or things are connected. An intimate relationship in an interpersonal relationship that involves physical or emotional intimacy and is usually mutually exclusive. The connotation of this word can vary from person to person, so it's important to find out what it means to the person you are dealing with.

For me, I was someone who loved the idea of being in a relationship, but I was nowhere near ready to actually be in one. From this I learned that it is very possible to want something, desire something, yearn for something in life that you just aren't ready for yet. And if you recognize this, great, because that means you can take the proper actions to get ready if it's really that important to you.

In the Beginning

Let's go back and look at our perfect world scenario. Let's presume that you've done the work required and you are confident that you are ready for the relationship phase. You are happy and content as a single individual, you are established and have all of your affairs in order, you don't have any negative weight lingering over you from past circumstances, you are an effective communicator, and you are dating with a definite purpose in mind. Now, let's say that as you explored the dating arena you end up finding someone that you feel is worth progressing with. You've dated for a few months, had engaging conversations, have chemistry based on mutual interests (not sex), and everythinghas been consistent. What happens next?

Well, if it's mutual and you are comfortable with each other, you can look to move toward the relationship phase. When entering this stage though, never forget how much effort you put into your dating phase. Not just the initial meeting part but the entire duration of going on dates and getting to know each other. If you are a guy—and a gentleman—I'm sure you pulled out all the stops. Opening doors, walking street side, fresh haircut before date night, suave outfit, compliments, flowers, paying for meals, etc. If you are a woman, I'm sure you were flirting, smiling, being polite and ladylike, engaging in genuine conversation, showing genuine interest, hair done, nails done, amazing outfit, and you may have even offered to pay once or twice on dates. For both of you I'm sure there was consistency all around (communication, etc.).

If you did all of this to get someone to like you, then why would you stop it when they do? The same thing it takes to get someone is what's going to take to keep them, right? That's the person they fell for, the person who was putting in the effort and showing appreciation. If you change that, you are changing the person they believed you were and, subsequently, the dynamics of what you've established so far.

One reason people stop putting in effort after the beginning stages is because they probably didn't set any follow-up goals. They have a plan on what to do in order to win someone's affection, but they fail to create a plan to keep it. What's the next step? Go into a relationship with the mentality that the beginning is just that—the beginning. Have a plan or goal for what you want to accomplish next. Never let the finish line remain in a fixed location.

When you keep the finish line moving forward, you give yourself a reason to be consistent with your actions and to exude effort. Another benefit of having this mentality in the beginning is habit setting. If you start off with a pattern of being consistent and putting forth effort, you are shaping the dynamic of what your relationship will be and subconsciously programming yourself to always playthat role. Whenthings gettough—and they will—it'll be a necessary habit to fall back on.

If getting them to like you or having sex with them is the finish line, then you have to be honest with yourself and reassess what your true motives were to begin with. In cases like this, it may have just been an infatuation that was satisfied after you accomplished your goal. Maybe your inability to see what's next means that they really weren't the one for you. Even in a perfect world we can still be persuaded by our less noble emotions (e.g., lust). But by following all the processes we've been covering so far and not rushing, this shouldn't happen too often.

Remember, the beginning of a relationship, even as far back as the dating stage, is where most of your dynamics will be normalized. That is, if you were true to yourself and what you wanted from then. Having a title shouldn't change things too much, so present maintainable expectations both for what you are offering and what you are willing to accept. It's not just effort and consistency but communication, affection, and boundaries as well; all of these are molded during these early times. As your relationship develops and evolves, some things may change, but these will always be there as the initial baseline and will typically be referenced as "how things used to be." So shape it purposefully.

As exciting as the beginning of a relationship can be, it can also be just as fragile. Everything is new, everything is heightened, and the potential goes all the way up to marriage! Being able to impact life on such a grand scale, it becomes a scary thing, and people can tend to overthink a lot. That's where its fragility comes from. Two people who were just strangers now thinking of sharing a life together. Giving your heart, trust, and future to someone or receiving them from someone should never be taken for granted. You have to appreciate the seriousness that goes into this decision, choosing each other, and hold on to that feeling for when ruts arise.

Getting to I Love You

Everything we've discussed so far has been a process right? Well guess what, stepping through the relationship once in it can still be a process. You have to continue to take things in stages and avoid the urge to rush it. Bask in the process as it grows and blossoms into something more beautiful each day. Don't accept a mentality that since we are in a relationship now, we have to accomplish every couple's goal imaginable in the next week.

If you went through the dating process properly, you would know your partner extremely well by this point. And the fact that you both agreed to be exclusive and form a relationship means that there must be heightened emotions on both sides. But that does not mean it has to be love. For some reason, many people believe that agreeing to be in a relationship with someone means you have to be ready to say, "I love you." These two things are very much capable of being independent of each other.

In fact, love gets thrown around so muchprematurely that it almost loses its potency. Unless you are really ready to say it based on your own individual criteria, don't let a title force you into saying it when it's not there yet. This means you'll have to respect each other's headspace. Everyone moves at different speeds, and if you just so happen to get there first, don't assume the other person is there as well. And if they aren't there in your time, be willing to accept that. On the other hand, don't feel obligated to say it back if it's not there yet.

What does love even mean to you? How strong of a commitment does it signify to you? Think about this: If you say it when things are still growing, then it's possible that you are attaching that level of importance to it. So as things continue to evolve or if something happens and you come to the realization that "now" you really love them, how can you express that when you've already burned that lamp. Now you have to change it up and say things like, "I love you for real, for real" or "I loved you, but now I really love you, I'm in love with you,"etc.

Just take your time getting to *I loveyou*. Let's get back to when saying those words actually meant something. I can tell you now—it is VERY hard to do. When you are around someone enough, sharing experiences and being intimate, and you have all these chemicals enacting on you, sometimes it wants to just slip right out. Discipline! Hold back until you know beyond a shadow of doubt you mean it. Develop some hard-hitting criteria for what it means to love someone and stick to it. Remember what we said in dating about how some words are just thrown around because they sound good. Don't let this phrase become one of those.

One thing I've learned through my relationships is that I will not say "I love you" until some point after we've successfully recovered from our first big fight. The reason is because personally, I feel that you don't really know someone until you've seen them in different states. Anyone can be amazing when happy, but seeing someone angry can tell you a lot about them. How much self-control they have, how they resolve conflict, what their true feelings toward you are, and their maturity level. And since reservation usually goes out the window when a person is angry, at this point you get a chance to glance behind another layer into who they really are.

My first wife and I never got into any fights prior to our marriage. Also, because she was pregnant, we rushed into it and really didn't get a chance to fully learn about each other. The day she left, we had just gotten into our first really big fight. I saw a side of her that to this day causes me to see her in a different light. If I knew she processed her anger like that, it definitely would've influenced the way I felt about her, and I wouldn't have pushed like I did for marriage. Not everyone may place the same weight as I do on this specific criterion but all the same, everyone should have something to use as a measurement in knowing when they are truly in love.

Love Goes in Cycles

When you do get to love, one thing you can rest assured of is that it goes in cycles. No matter how perfect a couple may seem on the outside, if you have a conversation with them, they will tell you that they have their share of ups and downs. But why? Yes, getting into arelationship for the wrong reasons or being with the wrong person can make these cycles more frequent, but there is something else to consider here. Foundation.

The more care, effort, and time you put into building a foundation, the stronger it will be. And having an immovable foundation is very important in getting through the down cycles. Meaning the times you feel like you don't like the person you are with, that will become the stronghold keeping things together. It's also what will remind you of why your relationship is worth fighting for and why you fell in love in the first place. It's where you can draw from in gathering the motivation to fight for your relationship. However, if you rushed, then there won't be much to pull from and the foundation may crumble during the low cycles.

A foundation can be constructed of anything, and it will vary from couple to couple. Some people are brought together by tragedy and that experience becomes their foundation. Some people are brought together by circumstance, others by mutual affiliation, so on and so forth. The common theme is that most foundations are built with some mixture of time and experiences. Understanding that lows are inevitable, make sure your foundation is ready to withstand them.

Another reason for cycles is the lack of goal-setting like we mentioned earlier. There is a quote that says, "If you aren't growing, you are deteriorating." Many couples, from what I've noticed, don't continually set goals as they progress as a couple. They don't even continue to have stimulating conversations. I've seen relationships where the people in them become zombies, just going through the motions but having no emotion. I'm sure you've seen them too—the couples at restaurants who can eat a whole meal together not saying a single word. When did they stop having those deep conversations that helped them learn about each other and paint goals for the future? Becoming a couple is the easy part. The hard work is what comes next—sustaining it.

Without consistently working toward something, a relationship can become stagnant. Stagnation can lead to death. When there is no growth being experienced, that's one of the criteria that can lead to down cycles and evoke thoughts like, *Why are we even together?* Goal-setting isn't just about planning the big things; you can set goals for small things as well. The important thing is working towards something together as partners in order to continually reinforce the bond you have.

One trick youcan use to combat the lowcycles, though it won't prevent them from occurring, is to adopt a "no way out" mentality. Take having the ability to quit and walk away completely off the table. As they say, "when you want to take an island, burn the boats" because you find untapped strength when your only options are to succeed or die. If quitting isn't an option, you are more prone to find a way to improve your relationship because the only other option would be to live in misery.

Just like with family, whether you are on good terms or not, they are still your family and nothing can change the blood you share. Your relationship's bond should be seen just like that blood tie. Unbreakable. Going back to foundation, if you did everything right, then you can trust that you are with the right person. Something in the process of getting into a relationship gave you that feeling that this was the one. That feeling is still there. You just have to find it underneath the present circumstances that are leading to the difficult times.

If you can't do that, then again, the person you are with may not be the one for you. Somewhere in your process you must've convinced yourself that you felt more for them than you actually did because when it's real, it's powerful, and there aren't many things that feeling can't overcome. Not being able to find it again requires an inner conversation with yourself. Try to determine if you were being genuine with how you felt and the things you really wanted from the beginning. By concluding that you may have forced it or rushed, an atmosphere is now created for someone to get even more hurt or damaged because now deeper feelings were invested by the other person.

Individual Growth Never Stops

Go back to the quote at the beginning of this chapter. You have to get proficient at falling in love multiple times but always with the same person. That's because people are always going through changes, and in a long-term relationship you will get to experience a few of them. When these changes start to occur, it will really depend on how well you know them fundamentally, which will determine the difference between you being able to see the same person and seeing somebody completely different. Because just as much as people change, there are certain core elements that will remain the same. And with those core elements embedded into your foundation, you'll always be able to see the person you fell in love with.

To better understand this, ask yourself the following questions. However old you are now, go back five to ten years and ask yourself: Are you the same person today that you were back then? Now, go back another five to ten years and answer the same question. What you'll find is that over the years you have evolved, matured, and probably encountered some shifts in personality and mentality. Essentially, you've become a new person. However, you may also realize that you still possess some of those base qualities that make you, you. Well, this cycle of change doesn't stop just because you get into a relationship. It continues.

You'll continue to grow and evolve, only now you have someone in the picture who may be affected by it. Just like some of your earlier changes may have caused you to bump heads with your parents, some of these changes may cause you to bump heads with your partner. Earlier, in relation to dating, I mentioned the things you establish during that stage become the expectation. Well, as you grow, some of those things could change, which means having to redefine new norms for your relationship. Anything organic is in constant change, and trying to reject it will only create chaos. You have to expect it, accept it, adapt to it, and move on into a new norm.

By preparing for these coming changes, you can put things in place to better handle them. Like, as I've been saying, making sure you build a crazy strong foundation, and making it even stronger during the good times. Taking every opportunity to reinforce base elements like love, trust, value, appreciation, being transparent, and open and honest communication are very important to accomplish this. However, even with a strong foundational bond, when change first arises, it may be accompanied by a little friction while the adjustment period takes place. But just like becoming a teenager and bumping heads with your parents didn't stop you from being their kid, neither should these growing pains stop you from seeing your partner.

So, understanding that change will be a part of your relationship, what should you do about it? One, you prepare for it by creating that stronghold for your partner's core attributes, character, and principles. The things that don't change that much over time. You accomplish this by allowing enough time upfront for them to be ingrained into the fabric of your relationship. Two, keep a clear line of communication with your partner and pay attention. By doing these, you'll become aware of when these changes are happening. Being aware allows you to better align yourself with the changes and create parallel shifts in yourself so essentially, you are evolving together.

This is my take on evolving together versus individually. Think of two masses moving parallel to each other with a rubber band wrapped around them. As long as they are moving in unison, the rubber band never experiences excess strain. Now imagine if they were both still moving forward, but now at a slight angle away from each other. How long until the rubber band reaches a point of being too stressed and pops? Well, the masses represent the people, the forward motion represents growth, and the rubber band represents the relationship. If you don't prepare for change, you run the risk of growing apart.

Who has heard someone around them say something along the lines of, "You've changed," "You aren't the same person I fell in love with?" "We just grew apart." Acknowledging that, yes, people can just blatantly change for any number of reasons or that a person never showed you who they truly were to begin with, more times than not, these statements are a result of partners not anticipating the natural time-driven changes people go through and/or adapting to them.

It's almost too easy to get caught up in the current snapshot of a person. Meaning the version of them you see in front of you right now. Right now, you are amazing! Right now, you are awesome! Right now, you are beautiful! Right now, you are funny, charming, etc. There is nothing wrong with appreciating those things; in fact, it's a must. But you also can't let those thingsbe what you base your emotions on because if they change, your feelings change. Focus on why are you amazing, why are you funny, why are you talented. Get to the core of where those things stem from and build your foundation there.

Getting to someone's core can't be rushed. Like an onion, it requires peeling back many layers. If you are already involved with someone and you are realizing that your foundation isn't as strong as it needs to be to overcome the down cycles, go back to the beginning. Go back and replay the development of your relationship to see what lies in the foundation. Sometimes in doing this, you are able to find new elements to add to the foundation, but other times you have to come to the reality that the relationship has run its course and you just have to be brave enough to accept whatever the outcomes may be.

Remember that severing a connection will always suck, but don't let the fear of experiencing that hurtful feeling convince you to stay. "There is no fix for being with the wrong person." I was the wrong person plenty of times, but there were still hurt feelings in the aftermaths. That's why the primary purpose of this book is to make sure you are really ready to enter a relationship and that you go about doing it the right way to minimize the possibility of you picking someone who isn't right for you or being the wrong person yourself.

Don't be afraid to have those conversations designed to feel the trajectory of the person you are with. Hard conversations can help avoid hard times. And yes, that includes the fear of having to lose what you've established so far and walking away. Always monitor how they are growing so you can either see if it's something you are willing to align with, or determine when it's no longer compatible or comfortable for you. Growth in any direction should be embraced because, again, if you aren't evolving, you are dying. In a true union though, more times than not, growth will be experienced together as two people will become one.

Please do not interpret this as saying there is no room for individuality. Of course, you have room to be your authentic and true self. Having your own identity is necessary for a relationship to thrive. I'm also not saying that you have to suppress areas of your growth just because you think it won't align with your partner's. Growing together as one simply means guiding your individual growth to still be in alignment with the overall success of the relationship. Have growth that is building you and your partner to the next level of life. If you start to experience growth that you can't alignwith your relationship, you'll start moving away from it.

After the Wedding Bells Stop

In a relationship, marriage is the ultimate goal, right? But what happens after you reach this milestone? What happens after the honeymoon phase? Do you consider it a job well done and leave it there? Or, like mentioned earlier, do you press forward to the next goal? For most people, it will depend on the type of person they are. Who were they in the past, and who have they become? For others, it will depend on how the relationship has been progressing up to this point. How fast or slow did things move? Is there already a trend of setting and achieving goals?

In my marriages, neither time was I really ready for that step. I realized that my only goal was to convince them to be my girlfriends. Everything that happened after that, because there weren't subsequent goals, was uncontrolled chaos. I was making circumstantial decisions based off what was happening, instead of guiding my decisions with a purpose.

In marriage one, we moved with no defined sense of purpose or plan, and she ended up getting pregnant. We didn't even know each other that well but decided to try and do the right thing. Everything was stacked against us to fail, and we did. Marriage one was over before it began, so other than the lessons on being patient with the process and really getting to know your partner, there wasn't much else I could draw from it. I do remember, however, after the pressure to get married and do the right thing was satisfied (after we got married), we looked at each other in a different light. That pressure that was influencing our thoughts was gone, and now we were just faced with looking at each other and realizing how fast we really moved.

In marriage two, there was plenty I had to learn from starting with the importance of staying consistent even after the wedding bells have stopped. Complacency kills. During our dating phase, I pulled out all the stops. We went everywhere and did everything. My goal was to convince her that she meant the world to me and that I was worthy to be her man. I succeeded. After we got married, that energy quickly started to fade away. All of those sweet things I was doing were cut in half, if not more than that, and we started having arguments over things that shouldn't have mattered if I was all in (i.e., other women).

All this stemmed from the fact that I didn't have a next goal in mind. I stopped working toward the marriage and became very complacent. Along with that came selfishness, inconsideration, disrespect, and a few other unbecoming behaviors from a husband. Yes, I can attribute this to simply not being ready, or like I alluded to earlier, not knowing how to be a husband, but I have to take responsibility for my part in it too.

When I joined my fraternity, they said the initiation was the easy part and that being in the organization meant the real work begins. My advice would be to look at a relationship, especially marriage, in the same regard. Getting someone to like you or be with you is the easy part. After you get them or marry them is when the real work begins. Make your partner a priority and it will influence the way you see and interact with them. Keeping that perspective in mind will even influence your decisions. Subscribe to the fact that whatever you did to get them, you have to do that and more in order to keep them because now they should mean much more to you.

Also, never stop looking ahead. Always have something you are striving for in your relationship.

Whether that's having kids, buying a house, taking a vacation, starting a business, or even planning a five or ten-year anniversary, keep having reasons to exert effort and keep moving forward.

Why This Book Matters

I mentioned that this book is for those seeking serious relationships, and everything up to this point has been an attempt to help you prepare for being in a successful one. With two failed marriages, I know what doesn't work. And with the time, study, and new practices I've developed, I understand better what does. Everything I've covered here consists of the things that I wasdoing that led to me failing and the things I discovered that have been helping me succeed.

I can't guarantee that doing any of this will make things perfect, or that they will even work for every situation. Because along with there being too many factors that have to be taken into consideration for each individual circumstance, this is also still just a single tool to try using against such a complex topic. Fill your toolbox with many more tools to have the best shot. However, by showing that you really want something healthy and happy, using this single tool is a way better start than doing nothing.

As of today, the divorce rate is 50 percent. And in black communities that number goes up to 64 percent.

When only considering black adults between the ages of twenty and twenty-five, the percentage is almost 75 percent. Doesn't that sound crazy? What happened to those relationships like our grandparents used to have? Though I can understand the sentiment behind that question, the fact is we are a different breed. Yes, we should strive for having a kind of commitment and loyalty as strong as theirs, but the times we live in make it much harder to get there.

For our grandparents, dating was completely different. They didn't have access to hundreds of singles. They were limited to those they went to school with or lived near. Also, opportunity was different back then, and being married helped to ease financial burdens as well as provided a degree of security in times when it was dangerous to walk certain places at night. Another consideration of those times is they had a sense of gratitude and pride in the simple fact of being able to marry and have a family in a country where those liberties were once disregarded.

For us, we are spoiled. We have access to people around the world and having access to so many options, no one feels obligated to stay with one person, especially if things get a little tough. Opportunity is also more abundant today, so most (I won't say all) people aren't looking at marriage to provide that sense of security. Living in a time where we can't fathom having a loved one ripped away from us and sold, in some ways, makes us take having someone who loves us and is there for us for granted. The I-can-do-bad-all-by-myself culture removes the need for resilience, and people would rather walk away than do what it takes for it to work.

People confuse effort with inconvenience when the reality is marriage is just hard, really hard, period. It takes a certain type of person to get through it, and that person comprises most of the qualities we've covered so far at a minimum. I'll be the first to say marriage isn't for everybody. If you feel that you "can't get it right," then regardless of how bad you want it, you may have to accept it's not for you. For instance, if you can't be selfless, understanding, empathetic, an effective communicator, manage responsibility, practice discipline daily, and/or are damaged in some irreparable way, then bowing out gracefully might not be a bad idea for now.

Despite the times we live in and the different motivations to go about getting into relationships, these characteristics are unchanging. That's why I believe this book is important. If enough people can fully understand this, relationships across the board should improve and my hopes are that divorce rates go down especially in black communities. I know that's a tall order, but it's what I want one of my contribution to society to be.

There are some questions you can ask yourself to see if you are meant for a relationship at this point in your life. When answering them, be honest with yourself and don't allow yourself to be swayed based on what you want.

1) Are you a selfish person?
2) Do you know what it means to love someone unconditionally?
3) Can you compromise on the things you want to accommodate a bigger picture with someone else?
4) Are you someone who can't admit when they are wrong or who can readily accept accountability?
5) Are you easily agitated? Do you get defensive often?
6) Do you have the ability to be patient?

Bonus Chapter

The Road After

I f you've done everything you can to make yourself a better person and you've gone through the dating process with a plan and a purpose but things still don't work out, what do you do? This is a reality that a lot of people are going to have to face. The answer is try again and don't lose any enthusiasm with the next person. Remember I said that being in a relationship is a skill. Well, it is and like any skill, it requires practice. You won't become an NFL player overnight, and you won't become a Picasso on your first art class. You have to keep doing it in order to get better at it. Some people may get lucky and hit a homerun the first time up, but I caution you against using anybody else's performance as a measure of your own. All of our paths are different, and all of the people we interact with will be different. However, if you stay the course, don't lose motivation and don't sway on your foundational principles that you've worked hard to instill in yourself. Eventually, you will find the one who will make it all worthwhile.

A common problem is that after a couple fails, people give up on the process. They figure it's not working and they let themselves revert back to old behaviors and old ways. DON'T LET THIS HAPPEN! Trust the process. In fact, after one relationship ends, before trying to get into the next one, take a moment to reassess and reaffirm who you are and what you want. Analyze what went wrong in this relationship and course correct for the next one. Remember don't use a new relationship as a band-aid for the last one. Fully process those emotions, like an emotionally mature person and move into your next relationship unburdened. There is no reason to rush, so pushing reset is ok.

Challenge

If you are in a relationship:

1. Take the love language quiz attached at the end of this book. Then, for thirty days, do something that feeds the love language you discover your partner has. It doesn't matter what scale (large, medium, or small) as long as it's purposeful and directed at the language.

2. Once a week (at a minimum) for two months, make it a point to sit down with your partner and have an in-depth conversation. The kind you used to have when you were dating. Often, we get so lost in the rapture of life that we stop connecting. Use this time to reconnect.

3. Set a goal that you want to accomplish as a couple. Make it very specific and give yourselves a deadline. Work together as a team to make sure you accomplish it. Use each other's strengths in this task, but also encourage each other's weaknesses.

If you are single:

1. Do an honest self-assessment on where you are
in life. Write down the ways in which you feel
you are ready for a relationship and write down
the ways in which you know you aren't. Use that
list to find the things you need to work on and
actually start working on them.

2. Start building habits and characteristics that
are beneficial to being in a relationship. Practice
effective communication techniques with your
friends and family so that it becomes a natural
part of who you are. Also, work on being selfless
with those closest to you. Even just having
these traits ingrained in you, your partner will
appreciate it.

3. Work on your discipline and self-control. Set a
goal that you want to accomplish over the next
thirty to forty-five days. Whether that's to do
something daily or refrain from doing something
daily, pick something that will provide a challenge
for you. Every thirty to forty-five days, repeat this
using the same or different tasks until you are
used to the discomfort that accompanies making
decisions and sticking to them at all costs.

Author Biography

Quinton D. McDonald was born and raised in Little Rock, Arkansas, on September 6, 1985. He graduated from John L. McClellan High School in 2003, then attended the University of Arkansas at Little Rock to pursue a degree in Business Administration. While there, he joined the prestigious organization Alpha Phi Alpha Fraternity, Inc.

Today he is a father, a Navy Sailor, an entrepreneur, and the author of *4 Children, 3 Baby Mommas, 2 Marriages Later*. Other works of his includethe children's book *Yes, You Are Beautiful Too!*, and *Dad, can I ask you a question?*, which both can be found on hiswebsite https://www.qmcdonald.com. When he's not wearing one of his hats, Quinton can be found at the one place that always brings him happiness: the pool hall. Playing since he was ten, I guess you could say he's a bit of a shark.

Quinton wrote this book because of his own experiences with relationships. As you can imagine by the title, not to mention the countless relationships not talked about, he went through a lot of failures before he learned what it takes to be happy. After his eyes were opened, he was able to recognize that the same behaviors he had were present in many people, which is part of the reason why being in relationships is so hard and divorce statistics are so high.

Quinton is driven by his desire to spread the lessons he learned in hopes of preventing others from experiencing heartbreaks or breaking other people's hearts like he did. One of the things he came to realize was simply that by being aware of certain principles or practices, a person could improve their behaviors in a relationship. This is part of his way to spread those things people need to be aware of in relationships.

If you would like to contact Quinton to inquire about speaking events, book signing, or ordering books in bulk, please contact him using the information below. Even if you'd just like to express your views on the book itself, he'd still very much love to hear from you!

Website: https://www.qmcdonald.com
Email: info@qmcdonald.com
Instagram: @prodigal_pharaoh
Facebook: https://facebook.com/qmcdonald06

Love Languages for Couples Worksheet

Gary Chapmanwrote the book *The 5 Love Languages*. In this book, Chapman suggests that each person has a specific way in which he or she gets his or her emotional needs met.

Most people have a primary and secondary love language (preference). Learning to speak their language can shift how you relate to each other. We often mistakenly believe that our partner or spouse speaks the same language we do and try to meet his/her needs using our language. This results in frustration and disappointment.

The 5 love languages are as follows:

Words of Affirmation

Verbal appreciation speaks powerfully to persons whose primary love language is words of affirmation.

Words of encouragement easily translate into love and support.

Quality Time

Many partners/spouses feel most loved when they spend physical time together doing activities that they love to do. Spending uninterrupted time together will bring a couple closer and, in the years to come, will fill up the emotional bank account.

Receiving Gifts

Some partners/spouses respond well to visual symbols of love. If you speak this love language, you are more likely to treasure any gift as an expression of love and devotion. People who speak this love language often feel that a lack of gifts represents a lack of love from their partner/spouse.

Acts of Service

Sometimes simple chores around the house can be an undeniable expression of love. Even simple things like laundry and taking out the trash require some form of planning, time, effort, and energy. Very often, both partners in a couple will speak to the acts of service language. However, it is very important to understand what acts of service your partner/spouse most appreciates.

Physical Touch

Many partners/spouses feel the most loved when they receive physical contact. For a partner/spouse who speaks this love language loudly, physical touch can make or break the relationship. Learn your partner's/spouse's "dialect" by finding his or her favorite acts of touch, whether it is hugging, kissing, holding hands, or lovemaking, and initiate it often.

1. Read these together with your partner/spouse.
2. Take note of which language is your primary and secondary love language.
3. Take note of which language you believe to be your partner's/spouse's love languages.
4. Discuss your love languages. Discuss which languages you believe are your partner's/spouse's.
5. Talk about specific ways that your partner/spouse can meet your needs using your love languages.

Made in the USA
Columbia, SC
31 October 2022

70262905R00109